BLARNEY CASTLE & GARDENS

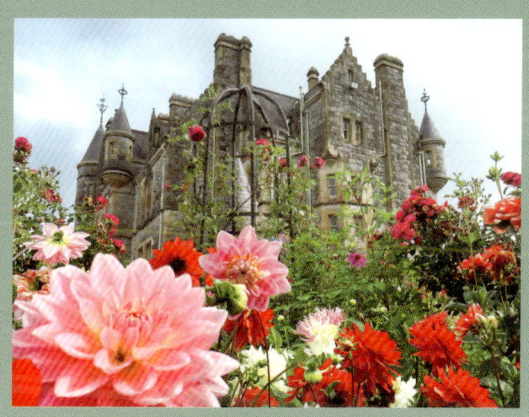

SCALA

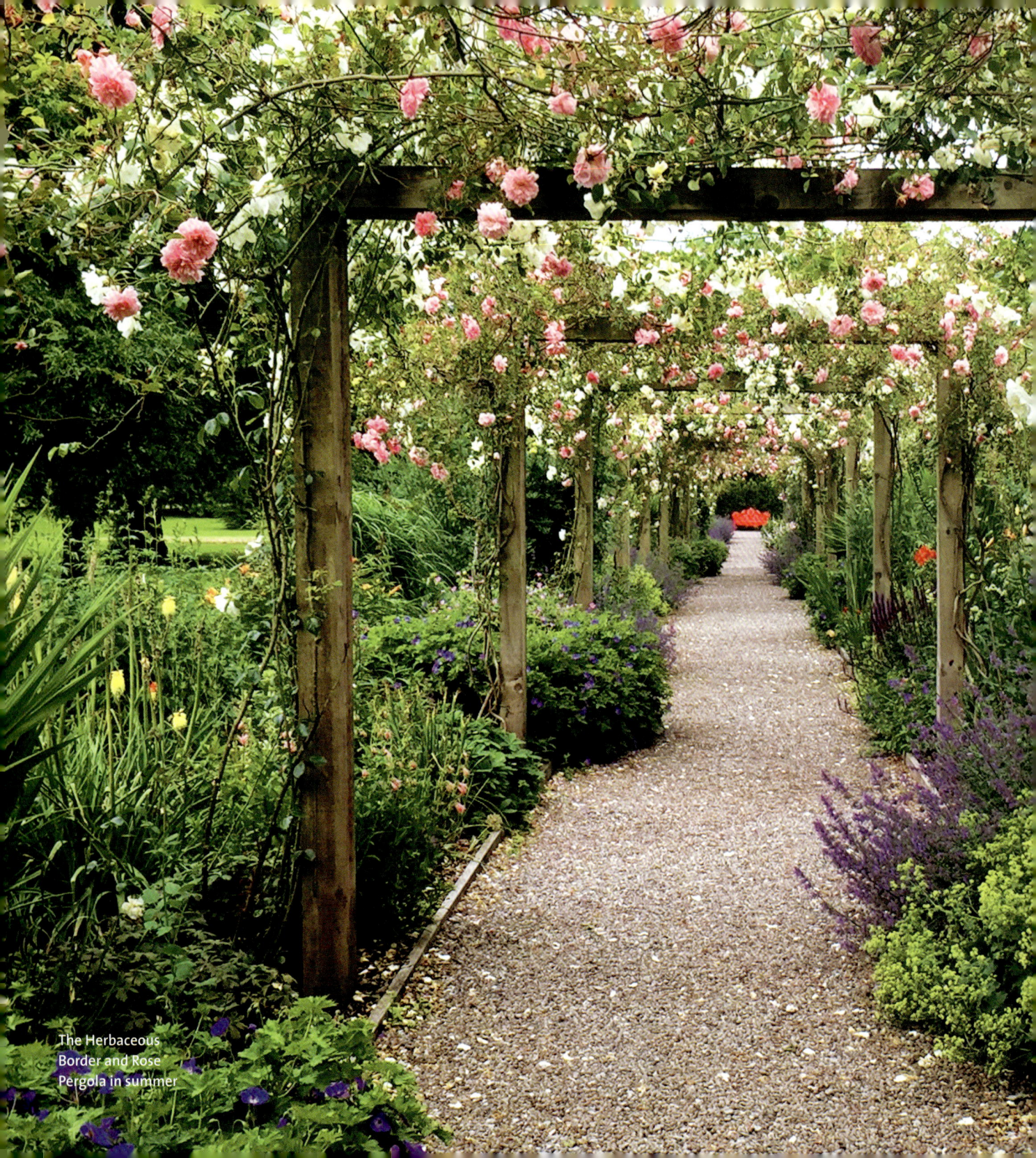

The Herbaceous Border and Rose Pergola in summer

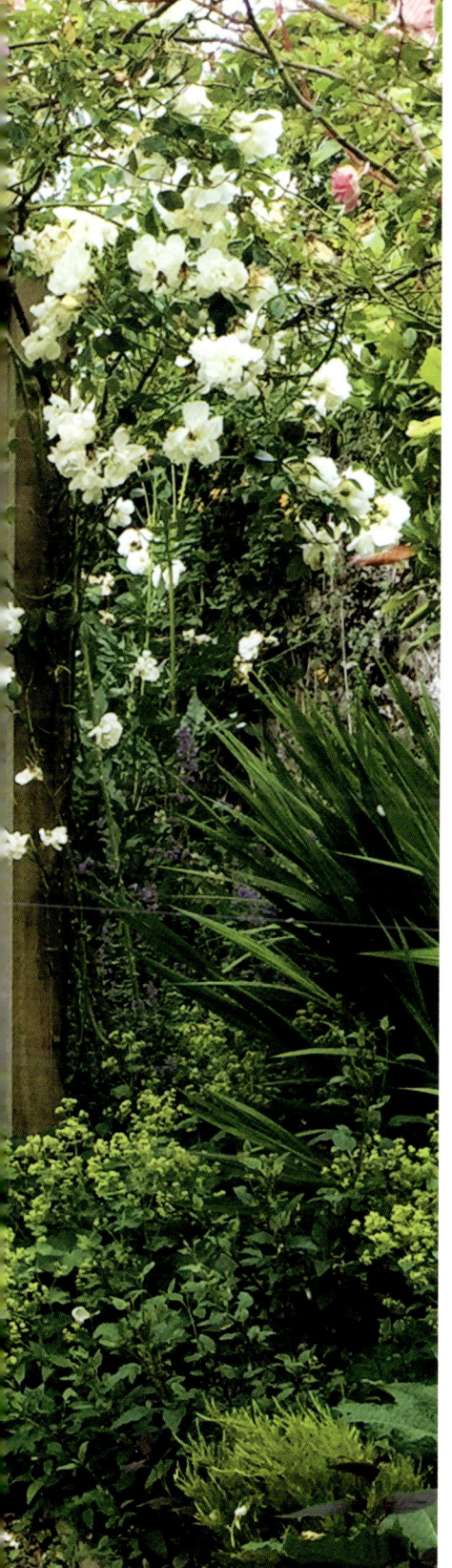

WELCOME TO BLARNEY

A warm welcome to Blarney Castle, Rock Close and Gardens, where we hope you enjoy your visit and take some time to explore.

The Castle as you see it today, is the third to have been erected on this site. The first, wooden building was erected in the 10th century AD. Around 1210 this was replaced by a stone structure with an entrance some 20 feet above the ground on the north face. To this was added, in 1446, the present keep in its entirety.

The Blarney Stone, the legendary Stone of Eloquence, is found at the top of our Tower. Here you may enjoy the unique experience of kissing the Stone and joining world leaders, famous entertainers and millions of visitors from around the world who have taken advantage of its magical powers to gain the Gift of Eloquence.

With the Castle surrounded by 60 acres of rolling parklands, no visit to Blarney is complete without experiencing our gardens, avenues, arboretums and waterways. Look out for Ireland's only Poison Garden, a touch of danger hidden in this beautiful setting. Discover the mystical wonders of the Rock Close, shaded for centuries by ancient yews, home in bygone days to hermits, druids and witches. The Gardens are full of delights and surprises, and their natural setting, ever-changing with the seasons, means that each visit brings new discoveries.

Blarney Castle Estate

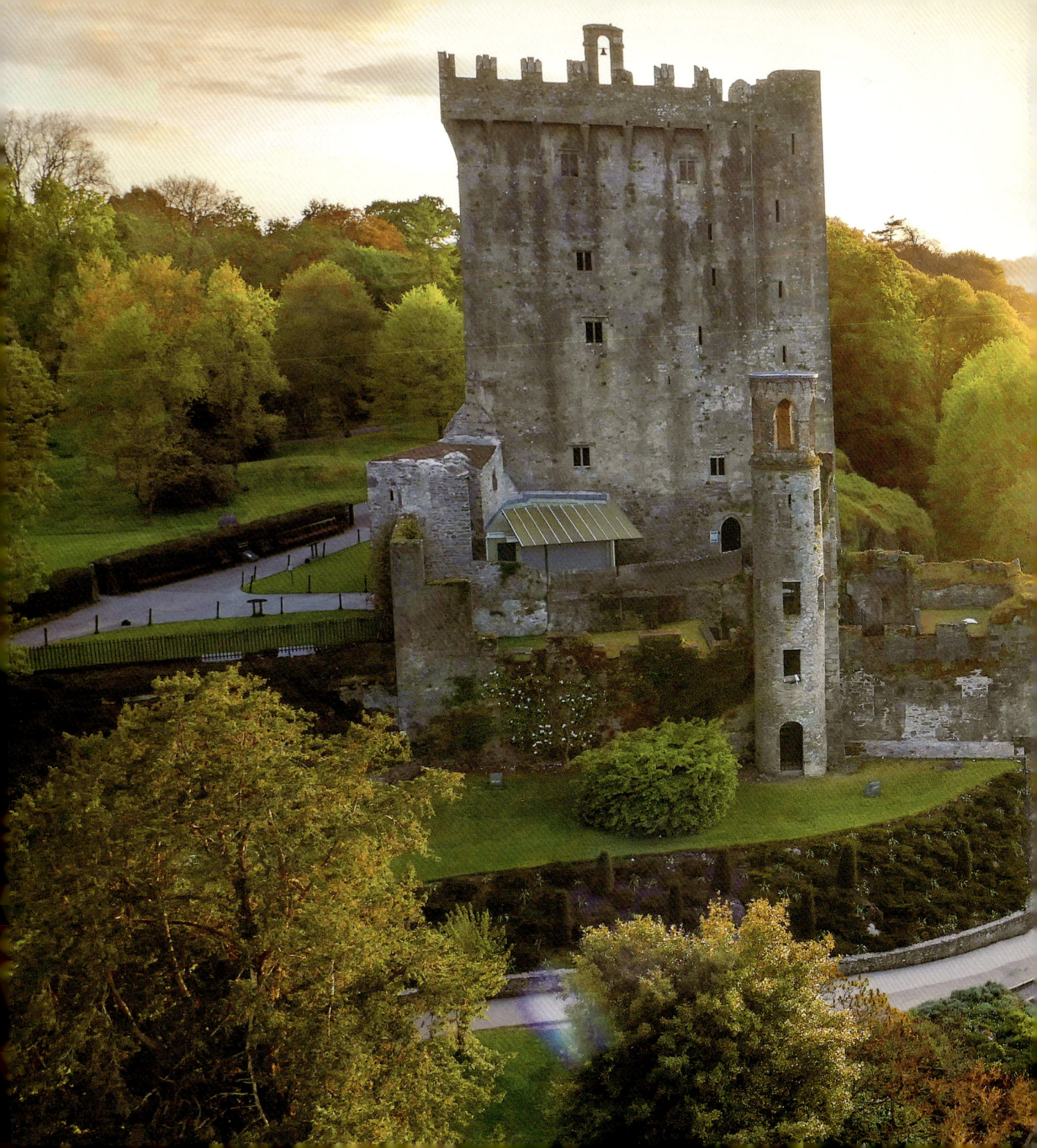

THE STORY OF BLARNEY

To visit Blarney Castle is to step back in time and feel the enchantment of a long and heroic past. The story begins nearly 900 years ago, when Ireland was ruled by clan chiefs. Blarney was the ancestral home of one of the most ancient and powerful clans of all: the MacCarthys

The MacCarthys reached the pinnacle of their power when their clan chieftain, Cormac, became King of Munster in 1127, more than three and a half centuries before his descendants built Blarney Castle. His seat was at the Rock of Cashel in County Tipperary, where he built the chapel on the rock which bears his name.

Later in the 12th century (1169) the Normans invaded Ireland and, although they adopted Irish culture and customs, they disrupted the old Gaelic lords' landholdings and political power, and introduced the interest of England into Irish affairs. Pope Adrian IV in the 1150s had granted Ireland to Henry II of England 'to erase its barbarism and secure its spiritual reformation'. Henry declared himself Lord of Ireland, distributed land to his Norman followers and sought the submission to his authority of the Gaelic chiefs from whom he took it. The MacCarthy Clan were early followers, submitting in 1172.

In order to retain their lands and power, Gaelic chieftains for the next five hundred years were constantly shifting allegiance, and were engaged in delicate political manoeuvres – none more so than the MacCarthys of Blarney; this ultimately gave rise to the legend of the Gift of Eloquence attributed to the Blarney Stone.

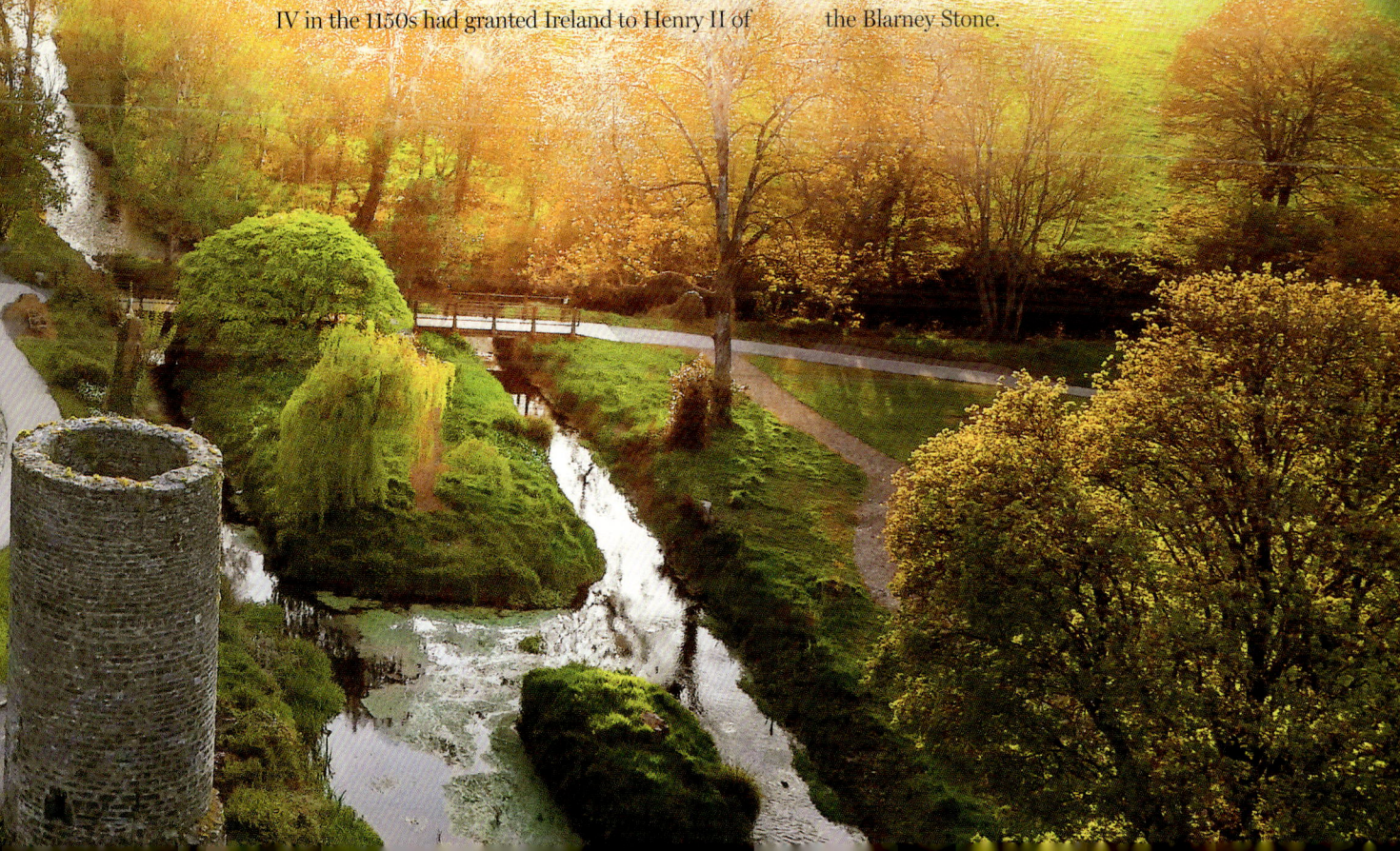

The first fortress

The resurgence of the power of the old Gaelic lords in the 14th and 15th centuries was marked in the case of the MacCarthys by the building of a friary and a castle at Kilcrea, south-west of Blarney. But most notably they built Blarney Castle itself. First a slender tower house was erected during the 1480s on a prominent outcrop of rock, possibly to fortify the Blarney valley, which they had reacquired in 1479. This now formed the most easterly part of their lands, which stretched westwards to the source of the River Lee, an area called Muskerry, hence their Chief was styled Lord of Muskerry. The Muskerry MacCarthys were one of the principal branches or 'septs' of the MacCarthy Clan, which ruled most of County Cork and part of County Kerry at this time.

Both Kilcrea Friary and Castle and the earliest part of Blarney Castle were built by Cormac McTaidhg 'Láidir' (Strong) MacCarthy, who died in 1494. It is thought that his son Cormac Óg (Young) Láidir McCormac MacCarthy added the splendid building we see today, early in the 16th century, as a declaration of the power and pride of this ancient family.

Reformation and rebellion

The 16th century saw the Reformation take hold in Europe and in Ireland, and here it added to existing political tensions. As Europe split roughly into Protestantism in the northern countries and allegiance to Rome in the south, the people followed the choice made by their leaders. Not so, however, in Ireland. The English administration, already struggling to keep control, now found that many of the chieftains and the vast majority of the people wished to maintain allegiance to Rome, despite the fact that all the bishops of Ireland had turned to the Reformed Church. As a result, the English were increasingly afraid of being invaded by their traditional enemies, Spain and France, via Ireland, aided by disaffected chiefs. Two centuries of strife resulted, more or less coinciding with the tenure of Blarney Castle by the MacCarthys of Muskerry.

In response to the danger of invasion, Henry VIII set about strengthening himself and weakening the great Irish chieftains. In 1541 he proclaimed himself King of Ireland (not just Lord as previously) and he introduced the system of surrender and re-grant of

Kilcrea Friary, County Cork

This friary was built for the Franciscan order in 1465 by Cormac McTaidhg 'Láidir' MacCarthy, who began the building of Blarney Castle. As well as a church, cloisters and domestic quarters, it contained a library and scriptorium where many manuscripts were produced by the monks, making the friary an important centre of learning. Thanks to the influence of the MacCarthys, it survived Henry VIII's dissolution of the monasteries in the 1530s and 1540s, but was sacked during the reign of Elizabeth I. The monks were allowed to return under James I but persecution continued during the 17th century. Its working life came to an end when the MacCarthys lost power at the end of that century.

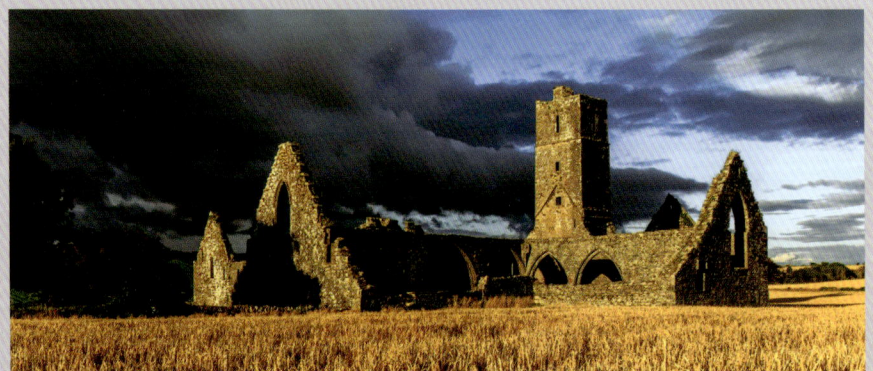

Few of the Friary's treasures have survived. A folio of manuscripts from its scriptorium is preserved in the public library of Rennes in northern France. A late 15th-century silver reliquary was found in the ruins, as well as a Renaissance ivory crucifixion figure from the Continent. It is recorded that when they sacked it in 1584, soldiers destroyed statues and pictures and fought over a depiction of the crucifixion embellished with silver and gold. All this hints at the richness of its furnishings.

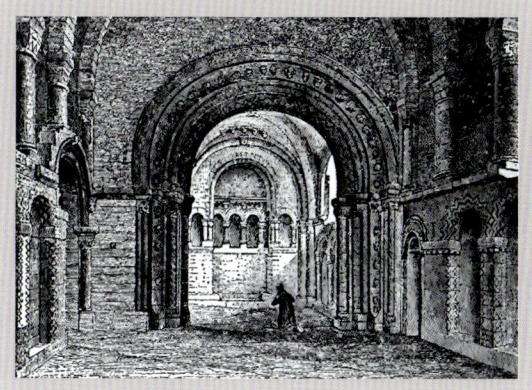

Cormac's Chapel

Built by Cormac MacCarthy, King of Munster, at the Rock of Cashel, Ireland's finest Romanesque building was consecrated in 1134. It was probably intended as the coronation church of the Kings of Munster.

lands, promising that the tenure of each chief would be recognised and defended by the central authority in Dublin against claims or attack from others. As his ancestor had done in 1172, Tadgh MacCormac Óg accepted this arrangement and in 1542 surrendered his lands to Henry VIII, who then re-granted them to him. On the surface all remained the same, but underneath there was a subtle shift in allegiance – and a major shift in legal status.

Henry also broke the power of the monasteries by dissolving them and taking their enormous land holdings, though Kilcrea was spared because of the influence of the Muskerry MacCarthys.

Hugh O'Neill and the Catholic uprising

Henry's actions, continued by his Protestant daughter Elizabeth I, led to rebellion by the Irish landowners. As a result, huge areas of land were confiscated by the English Crown and later planted with English Protestant families, thus weakening the old Gaelic order. However, the great leader of Gaelic Ireland, Hugh O'Neill, Earl of Tyrone, united many of the lords and with help from Spain planned to defeat the English in Ireland and be rid of English interference. This was the situation that Cormac MacDiarmada found himself dealing with, having only recently surrendered and been re-granted his lands from the Crown. He wrote to Sir Robert Cecil, one of Queen Elizabeth's closest advisors, 'from my house at Blarney', outlining the sacrifices he had made and the battles he had fought on the Queen's behalf, and assuring him that he had now refused to join O'Neill's uprising. Yet Cecil then learned that MacCarthy's kinsmen and followers had joined O'Neill as he marched through Muskerry on his way to meet the Spanish forces, due to land at Kinsale. This caused the English (and perhaps the Queen herself) to declare that MacCarthy's letters 'were all Blarney'. Hence the famous usage of the word had its origin in a very real dilemma.

In the event, when the fateful battle took place, Cormac MacDiarmada MacCarthy fought on the side of the English.

O'Neill was defeated, the Spaniards left, and the Battle of Kinsale, fought in 1601, sounded the death knell for Gaelic Ireland. However, Cormac MacDiarmada was able to return to Blarney where he lived until his death in 1616. He was the last Lord of Muskerry to be buried at Kilcrea Friary.

Hugh O'Neill, Earl of Tyrone (1540–1616)

Rebellion and the Jacobites

The reign of James I (1603–25) was relatively tranquil, notable mainly for the expansion of English Protestant settlers on land confiscated from the lords who had supported O'Neill's uprising. Ireland was losing its language and its customs, and the remaining Gaelic lords such as the MacCarthys had to adapt. Indeed, Cormac MacDiarmada's son, Cormac Óg, took the English title Viscount Muskerry. It was probably he who expanded Blarney Castle, building a Jacobean-style house onto its eastern side and enlarging windows in the tower itself.

In 1625 Charles I succeeded James I and in England tensions grew between him and his Parliament. In Ireland his unkept promises to ease anti-Catholic laws convinced many that rebellion was the only answer, under cover of the Civil War that had broken out in England. The Catholic lords, having created a Confederacy, attacked and persecuted Protestant settlers. At Blarney Donnachadh MacCormac Óg, 2nd Viscount Muskerry, became a leader of the Confederacy and caused Richard Boyle, 1st Earl of Cork, to declare all MacCarthy landowners in Cork outlaws. In 1646 Blarney Castle was attacked and fell to Parliamentary forces led by Lord Broghill, a son of the Earl of Cork.

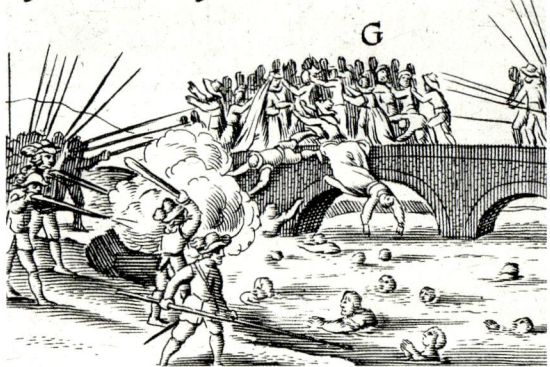

The massacre of English settlers by Irish rebels, October 1641

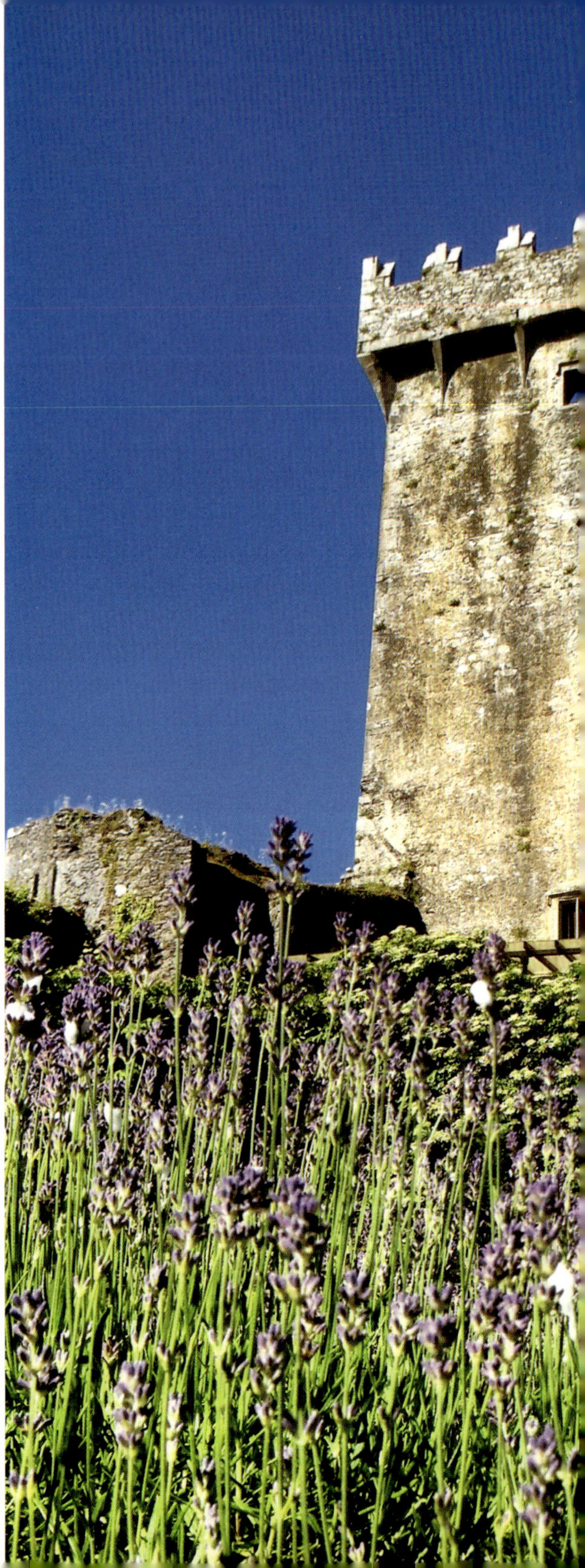

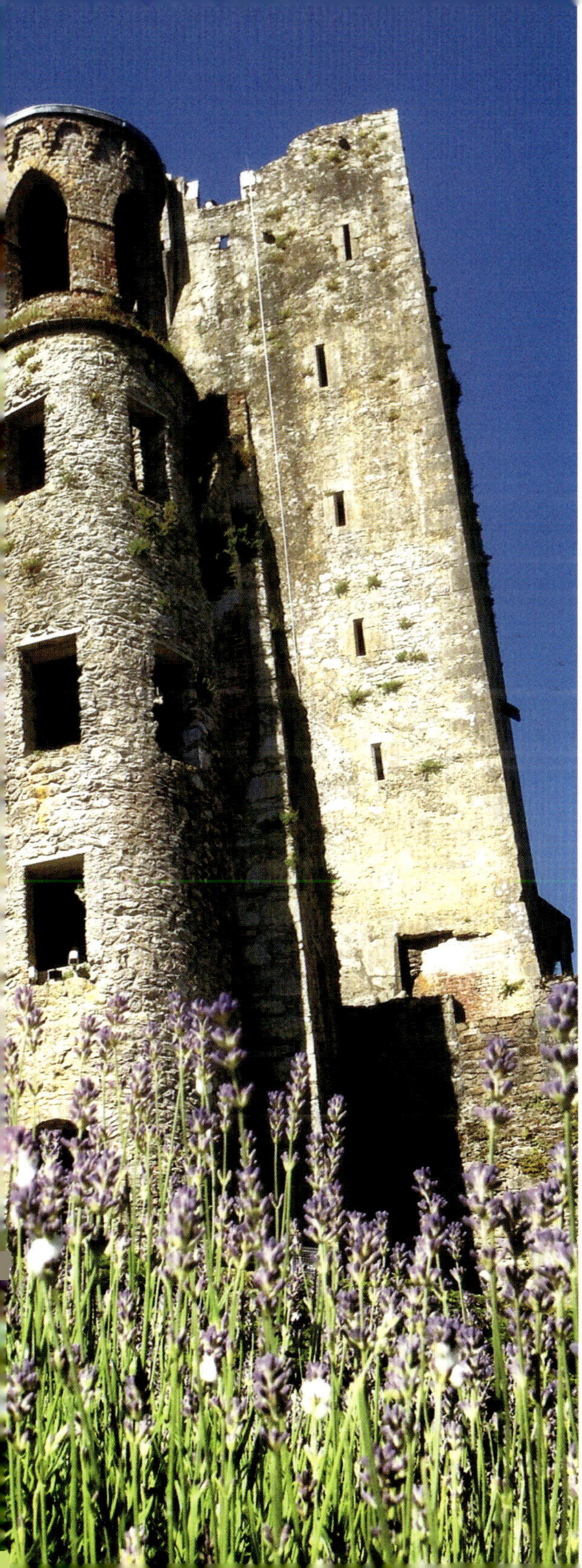

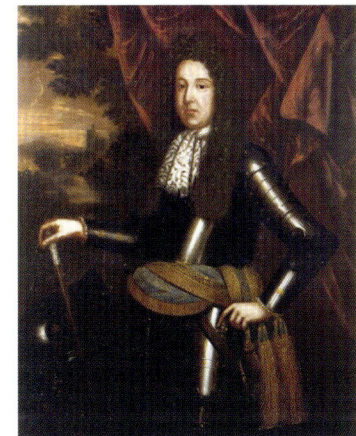

Donnachadh MacCormac Óg, 2nd Viscount Muskerry (1594–1665)

As soon as the Civil War in England ended in 1649, with victory for the Parliamentarians over the forces of Charles I (who was executed), Cromwell, Lord Protector of England, came to Ireland to subdue the Catholic chieftains. Kilcrea Friary was attacked and destroyed by his forces. Donnachadh MacCormac Óg, 2nd Viscount Muskerry, was one of the last to surrender, in 1652. Blarney was confiscated and granted to Lord Broghill. Muskerry fled to France, where he joined the exiled court of the Stewarts, headed by Charles II, and was created Earl of Clancarty in 1658. In one of the great twists of history, Charles II was restored to the throne in 1660, and he in turn restored Donnachadah, now Earl of Clancarty, to Blarney and the greater part of his estate.

Clancarty died four years later, in 1665. Sadly, his son Charles, Lord Muskerry, had been killed in a naval engagement only a month before. His heir, Charles James, was just a baby. He in turn died aged three or so, and therefore the inheritance moved sideways to a brother of Clancarty, at that time studying in a French seminary to become a priest. He returned to Ireland as the 3rd Earl of Clancarty.

The end of an era

On returning to Ireland, the 3rd Earl married a daughter of the Earl of Kildare, a Protestant. He and his heirs continued to support Protestantism, at least outwardly, until the accession of James II, a Roman Catholic. During the siege of Elizabeth Fort in 1690, when Cork had been taken over by Roman Catholic supporters of King James and Protestants were imprisoned in the city, Clancarty made Blarney available as a prison for the overflow.

But James II lost and Clancarty was imprisoned in the Tower of London. In 1694 he escaped to France, where he and other fleeing Irish joined the ranks of the Wild Geese. The MacCarthys had left Blarney for the last time.

The Jefferyes: a new age of prosperity

Meanwhile, in 1702 Blarney Castle was purchased by the Hollow Sword Blade Company of London. The company sold it, plus 1,401 acres, to the Lord Chief Justice of Ireland Sir Richard Pyne, for £3,800 in April 1703. Fearful of a MacCarthy return, he then resold it the following year to the Governor of Cork City, Sir James Jefferyes. It was the Jefferyes family who had the 17th-century house attached to the Castle almost entirely demolished and in its place built a Georgian 'gothick' house of grand proportions.

James St John Jefferyes, grandson of the first Sir James, inherited the Castle at the age of six in 1739. He was one of the principal introducers of the Industrial Revolution to Cork, indeed to Munster. He was also active in improving the roads and building bridges around Blarney. One of these was known as the Dry Bridge, which was beautifully

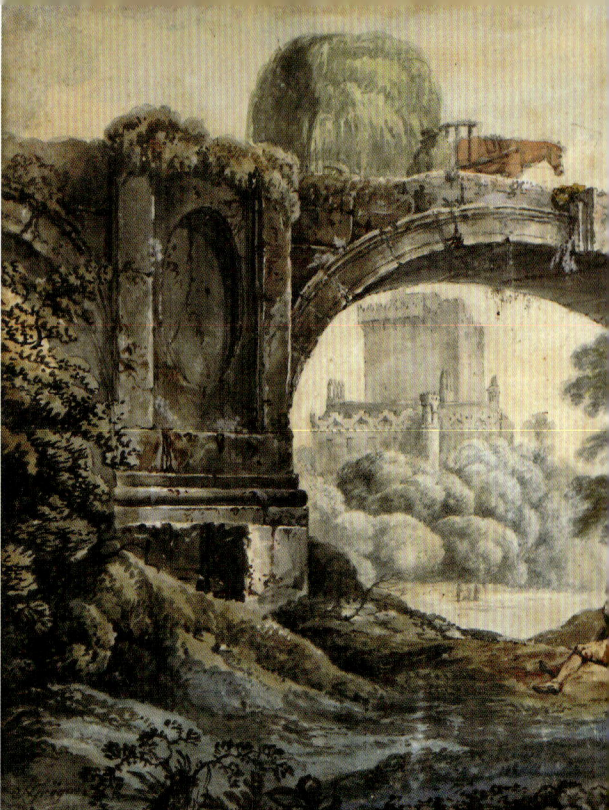

RIGHT Nathaniel Grogan, *The Dry Bridge at Blarney*, 1790

BELOW Gabriel Beranger's drawing of Blarney Castle, c.1775–7, showing the Georgian 'gothick' mansion built by the Jefferyes family

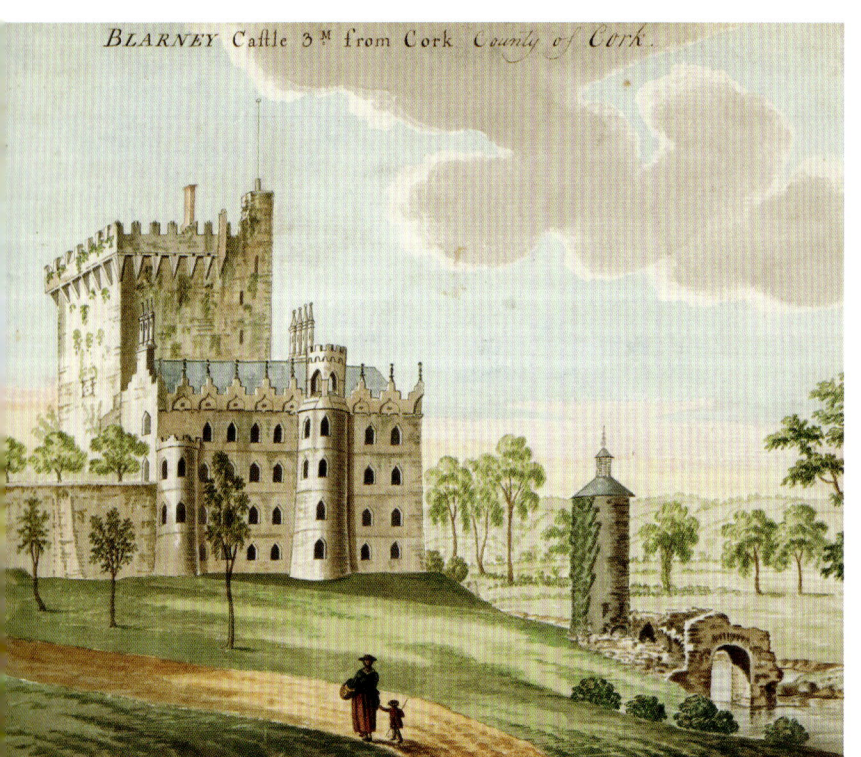

designed, with embellishments in the classical style, and could be seen from the windows of his mansion.

Jefferyes's project to bring prosperity to Blarney was such a success that within ten years there were more than 30 mills of various types here: a large stamping mill (for printing patterns), bleaching mills, stocking mills, woollen mills, paper mills and ancillary structures such as tucking mills and 'gigg' mills (both for finishing and smoothing cloth). The new Blarney attracted visitors not just to see the Castle but to see the great waterwheels turning and to note the prosperity of the men, women and children who lived and worked there. Fathers, sons and daughters worked in the mills, and the factory hooter told the village when it was time for lunch.

A romantic idyll

The Castle grounds remained open to members of the public who wished to enjoy them. When Charles Smith published his *Ancient and Present State of the*

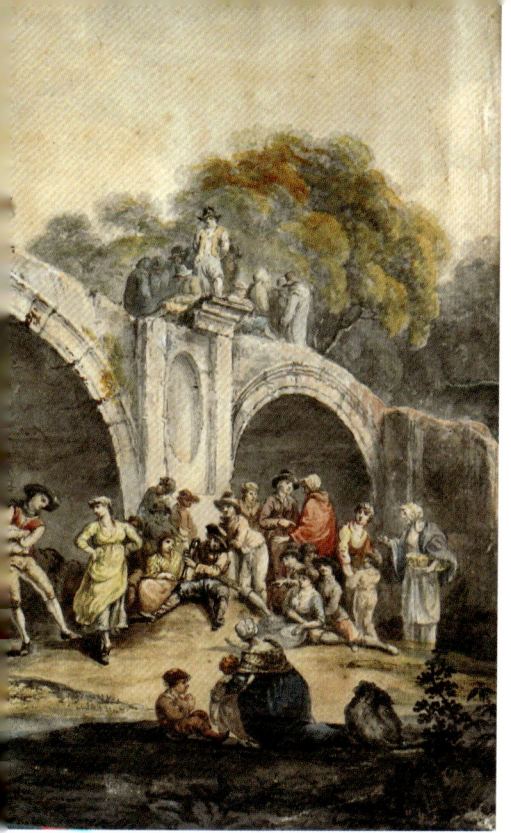

County and City of Cork in 1750 he said of Blarney: 'Adjoining to this castle, is a fine park, sweetly wooded, and well watered; also a fair bridge over Blarney river. The gardens of the castle are well laid out and kept in good order.' The Jefferyes family added further attractions, such as the two folly-towers on either side of the Castle. Most notably, though, they took advantage of the weathered outcrop of rock to the east of the Castle to create a fantastic landscape, including a druidic sacrificial altar and other grotesque features beneath the branches of ancient yew trees, the roots of which cling to giant boulders and the rock itself. Blarney now became a place of romance and began to be celebrated in myth and poetry, whilst remaining symbolic of an Ireland now lost forever.

After a devastating fire in 1820 – some say the result of a family squabble and to stop the then heir from inheriting it – the family moved out but retained possession of the estate, and the Castle with its attendant ruins developed a forlorn look.

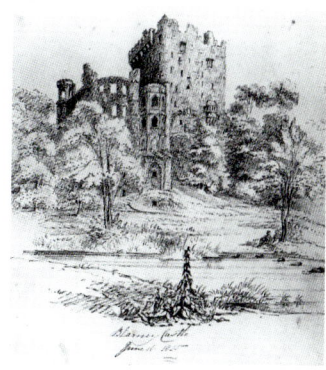

Pencil drawing of Blarney Castle by S.M. Derinzy, June 1825, with the burnt-out ruin of the Jefferyes family's mansion

The model village

James St John Jefferyes was an 'improving landlord', determined to bring prosperity to the people of Blarney. From 1765 onwards he set about transforming Blarney into a model estate village, one of the finest in Ireland. He took advantage of the abundant streams, able to power mills, to entice industry into the area. But he did much else. Arthur Young, in the mid-1770s, tells us that 'in 1765, when Mr Jefferyes began to build this town, it consisted of only two or three mud cabins; there are now ninety houses. He first established the linen manufactory, building a bleach-mill, and houses for weavers etc., and letting them to manufacturers from Cork'.

Following the principle of good design, Jefferyes's model village forms the heart of Blarney today. Ninety neat stone houses with slate roofs and long gardens were laid out on three sides of a bleaching lawn, now the village green, and were let out to textile manufacturers from Cork who wove cotton and linen yarn into cloth. His church still overlooks the green and its separate entrance for the family on the north side remains, together with their box pew in the north gallery with its fireplace, now used as a meeting-room.

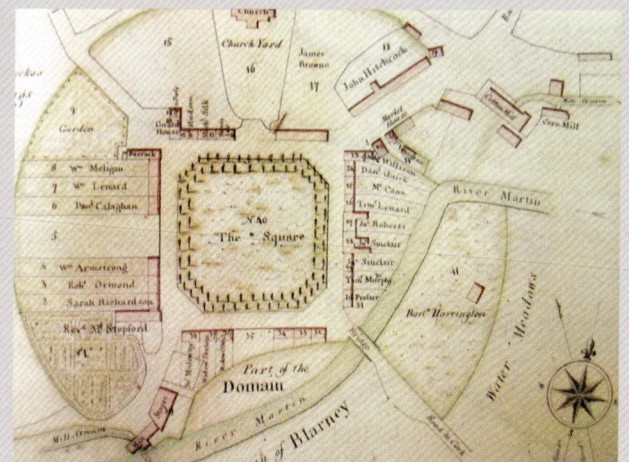

Plan of Blarney Village in 1801 by David Aher

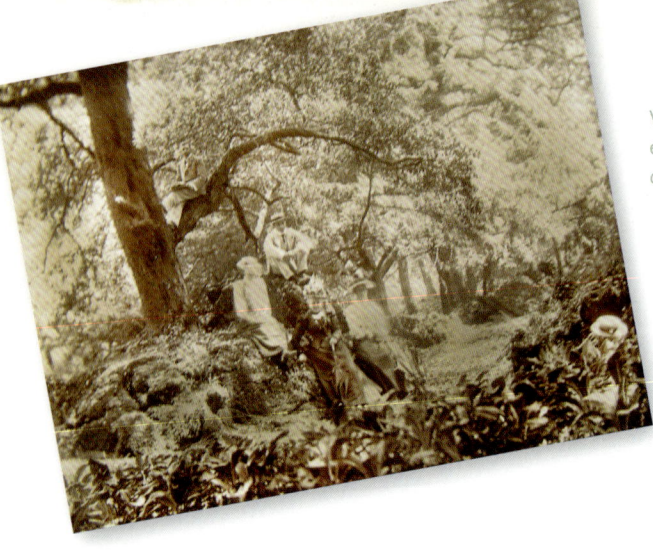

Victorian visitors enjoying the Groves of Blarney, 1899

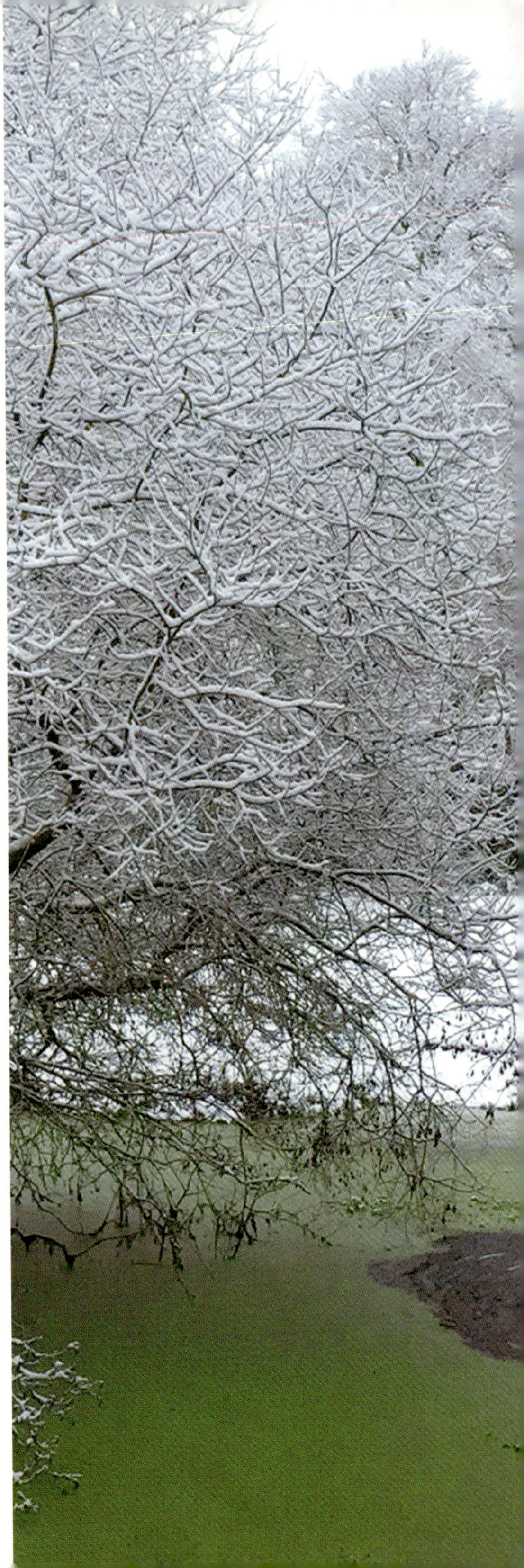

THE GROVES OF BLARNEY

by Richard Alfred Millikin

The groves of Blarney,
They look so charming,
Down by the purlings
Of sweet silent brooks,
All decked by posies
That spontaneous grow there,
Planted in order
In the rocky nooks.
'Tis there the daisy,
And the sweet carnation,
The blooming pink,
And the rose so fair;
Likewise the lily,
And the daffodilly —
All flowers that scent
The sweet open air.

'Tis Lady Jeffers
Owns this plantation;
Like Alexander,
Or like Helen fair,
There's no commander
In all the nation,
For regulation
Can with her compare.
Such walls surround her,
That no nine-pounder
Could ever plunder
Her place of strength;
But Oliver Cromwell,
Her he did pommel,
And made a breach
In her battlement.

There is a cave where
No daylight enters,
But cats and badgers
Are for ever bred;
And mossed by nature
Makes it completer
Than a coach-and-six,
Or a downy-bed.
'Tis there the lake is
Well stored with fishes,
And comely eels in
The verdant mud;
Besides the leeches,
And groves of beeches,
Standing in order
To guard the flood.

There gravel walks are
For recreation,
And meditation
In sweet solitude.
'Tis there the lover
May hear the dove, or
The gentle plover,
In the afternoon;
And if a lady
Would be so engaging
As for to walk in
Those shady groves,
'Tis there the courtier
Might soon transport her
Into some fort, or
The 'sweet rock-close'.

There are statues gracing
This noble place in —
All heathen gods,
And nymphs so fair;
Bold Neptune, Caesar,
And Nebuchadnezzar,
All standing naked
In the open air!
There is a boat on
The lake to float on,
And lots of beauties
Which I can't entwine:
But were I a preacher,
Or a classic teacher,
In every feature
I'd make 'em shine!

There is a stone there,
That whoever kisses,
Oh! he never misses
To grow eloquent.
'Tis he may clamber
To a lady's chamber,
Or become a member
Of parliament:
A clever spouter
He'll sure turn out, or
An out-and-outer,
'To be let alone',
Don't hope to hinder him,
Or to bewilder him;
Sure he's a pilgrim
From the Blarney stone!

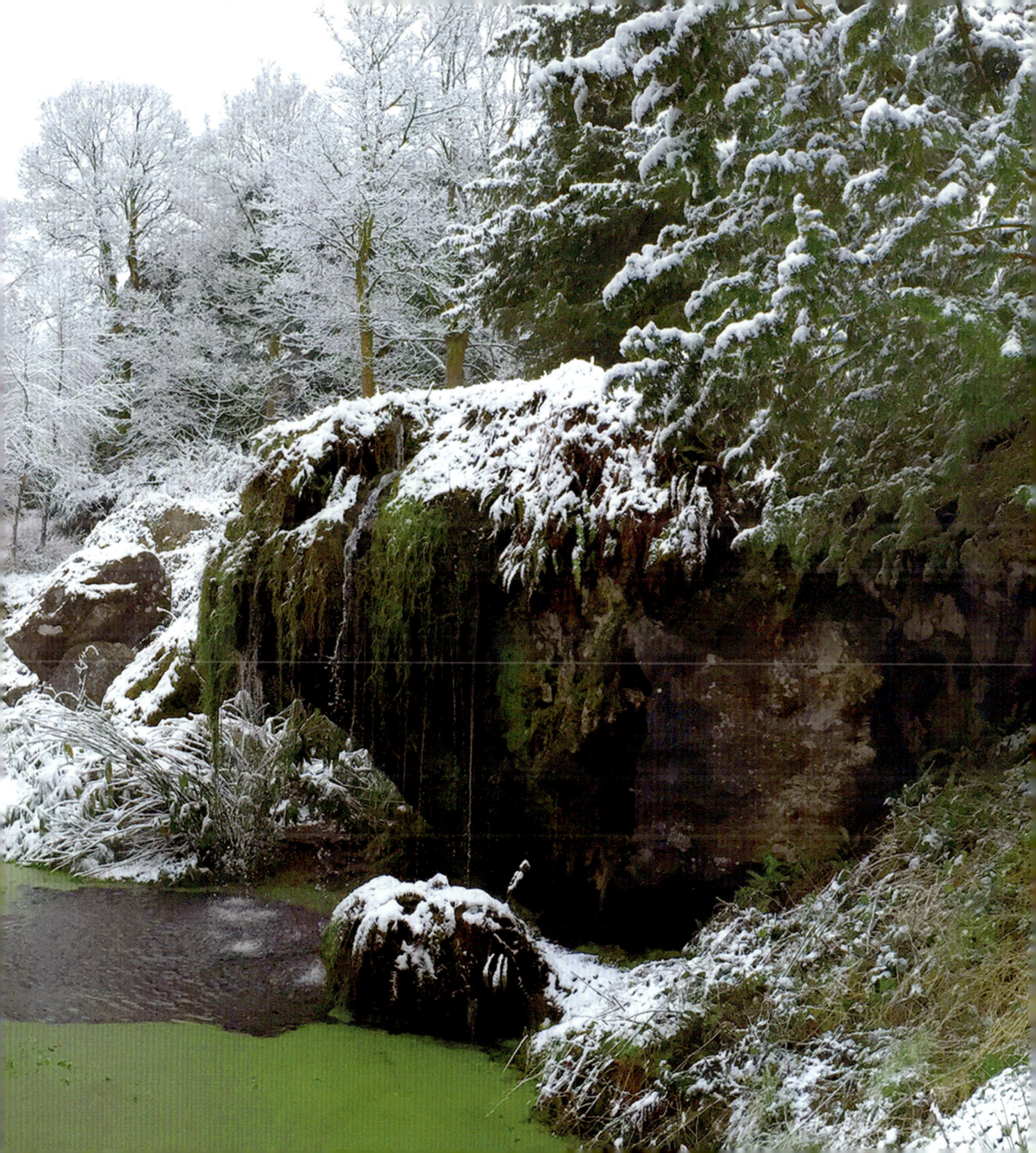

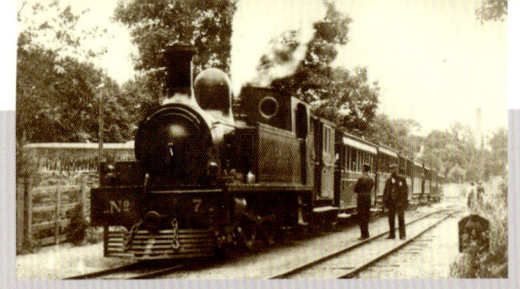

The Cork and Muskerry Light Railway

The narrow gauge railway connecting Cork City with Blarney Village was known as the 'Blarney Tram' or the 'Muskerry Tram' because it ran along the road from Cork. The line was built with investment from local landowners, eager to capitalise on the growing tourist industry. The station can still be seen near the entrance to the Gardens.

The railway opened with much celebration on Monday 8 August 1887; on the following Sunday nearly 2,000 passengers travelled on excursion trains to a sports meeting in Blarney. As demand increased, the line extended to Coachford and Donoughmore and was soon carrying not only tourists and day-trippers, but local passengers, livestock and farm produce.

The Tram was not known for its speed: one regular schoolboy passenger, who ended his career as a Catholic bishop in Honolulu, recalled that he thought the train was going quite fast until he looked out of the window and saw it being overtaken by a donkey and cart at full trot. Every September a notice appeared in the carriages saying: 'Passengers are requested not to pick blackberries while the train is in motion'! The slow speed of the train did not entirely prevent accidents: in 1927 it was derailed when it collided with a steam roller.

Eventually the much-loved little railway was beaten out of existence by competition from road transport, and the last train steamed out of Cork on Saturday 29 December 1934.

The Golden Age of travel

With improved transport links, Blarney soon became a popular destination for visitors from the USA disembarking from ocean liners in Cork Harbour, and, later in the century, arriving by air. Day-trippers by road and rail now came to Blarney in their thousands, eager to sample the delights of Blarney – and of course to kiss the Blarney Stone. Contemporary travel posters often featured the familiar silhouette of Blarney Castle.

*Ireland,
Land of Romance*
by G.H. Bland,
c.1930

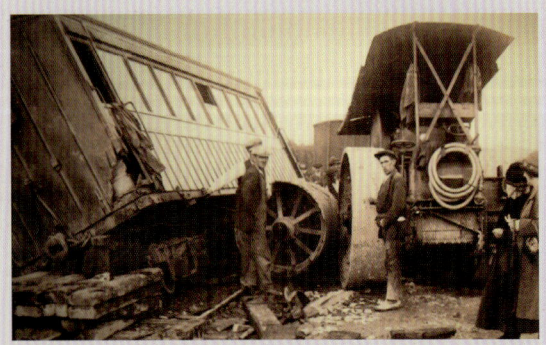

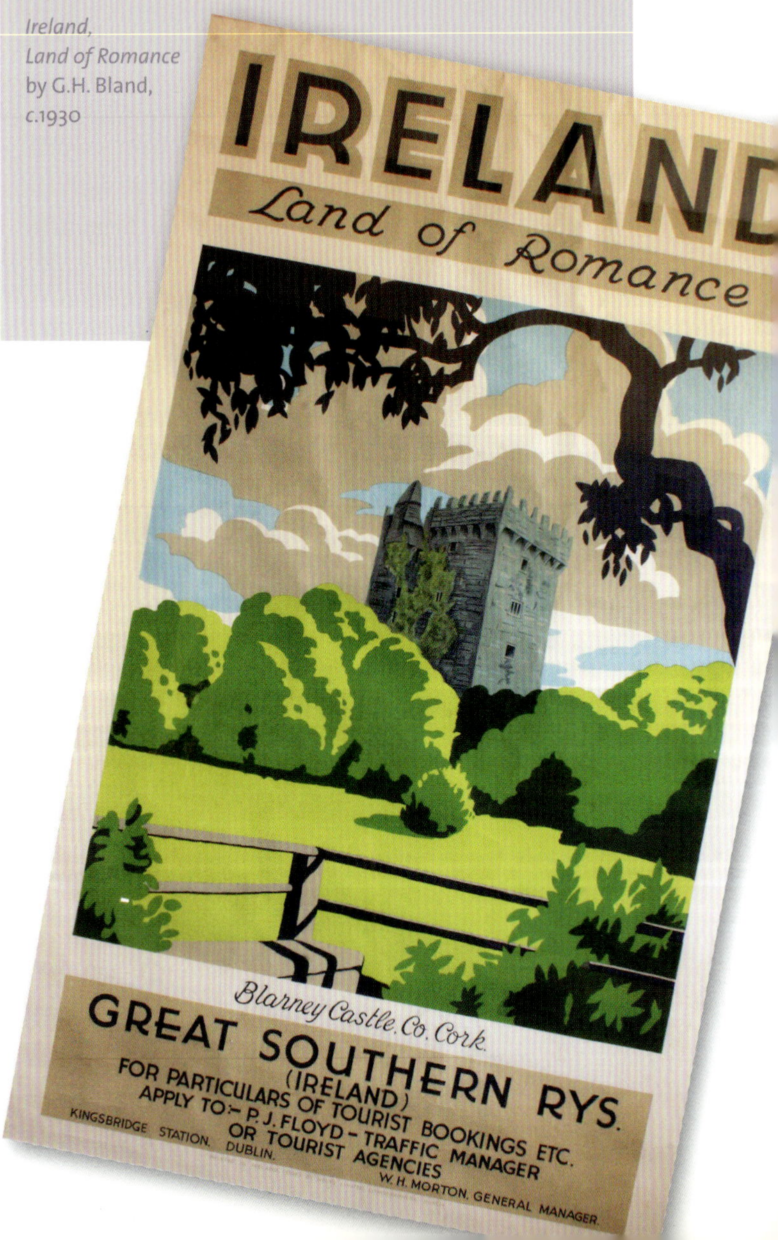

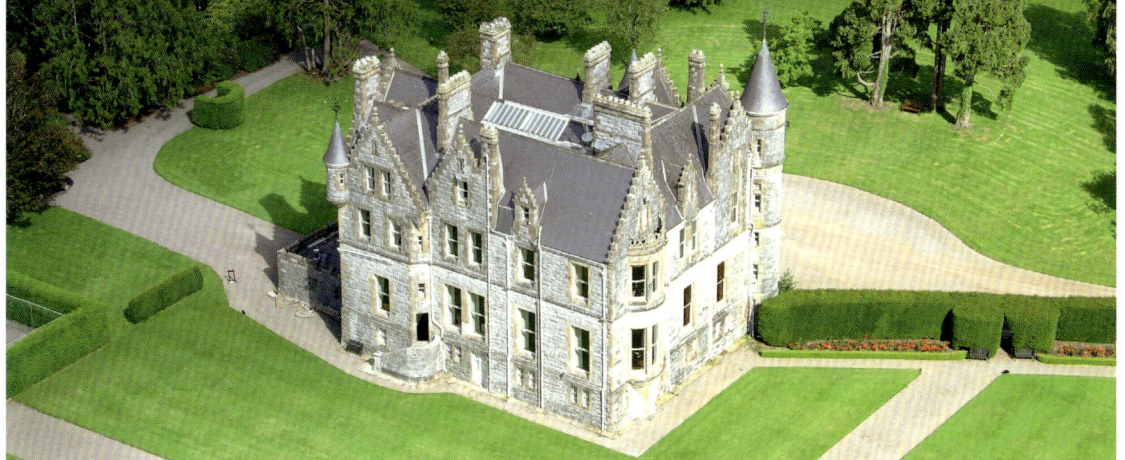

Blarney House today

The Colthursts: Blarney today

In 1846 Louisa Jane Jefferyes married a neighbour, Sir George Colthurst of Ardrum, just west of Blarney, and the Blarney estate passed to the Colthurst family. But they did not return to Blarney until 1874, when they built a new Scottish baronial mansion a few hundred yards south of the Castle, overlooking Blarney Lake. This is the present home of Sir Charles Colthurst, 10th Baronet.

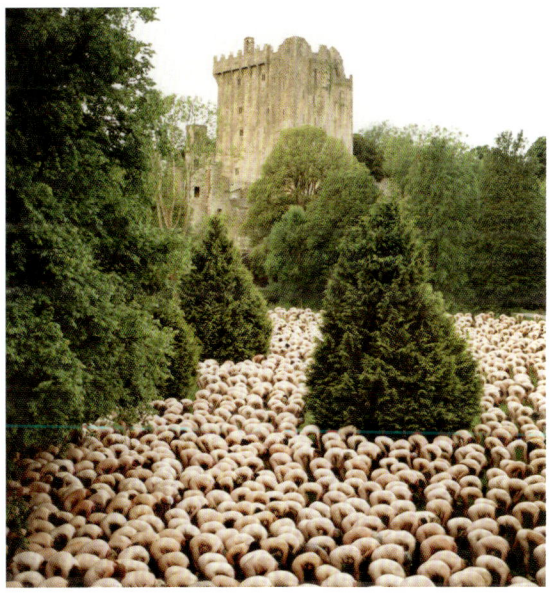

Spencer Tunick installation in front of Blarney Castle, 17 June 2008

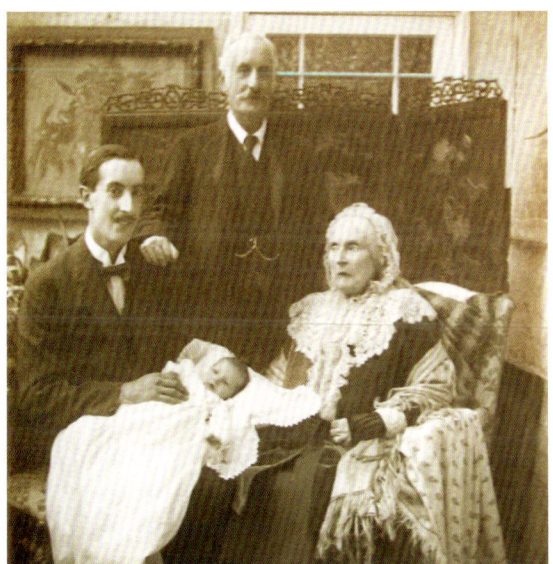

Four generations of Colhursts in 1912: Dowager Lady Louisa Colthurst (*née* Jefferyes) with her son, Sir George Colthurst, her grandson, Richard Colthurst, and her great-granddaughter, Mary Penelope

In the 18th century the Jeffereyes managed the Rock Close using the natural limestone and yew trees. This has been added to by the Blarney Estate on an ongoing basis, with a huge array of exotic and native trees, Poison Garden, fernery and pergolas. It is this estate which hosts a number of events each year. For instance, in 2008, as part of the Cork Midsummer Festival, very early in the morning the American photographer Spencer Tunick, photographed a crowd of 1,100 people in various places in and around the Castle – all of them totally naked.

THE MYSTERY OF THE BLARNEY STONE

The term 'blarney', meaning beguiling but misleading talk, gained currency during the 16th century as the MacCarthy of the day attempted to fend off the demands of Queen Elizabeth I. But it was not until the late 18th century that this quality attached itself to a stone in the Castle – just as Blarney was beginning to become a popular place to visit.

Legends about the Stone's origin emerged, each as plausible as the next. It was said to have been the stone used by Jacob as a pillow when he dreamed of the ladder extending up to heaven with angels ascending and descending on it, and that it was brought from the Holy Land after the Crusades.

'There is a stone there, That whoever kisses, Oh! He never misses, To grow eloquent.'

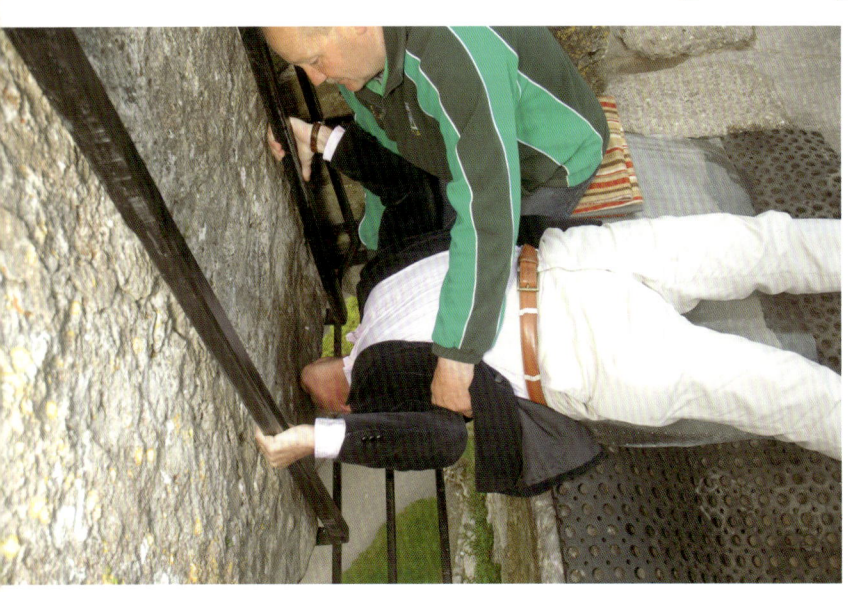

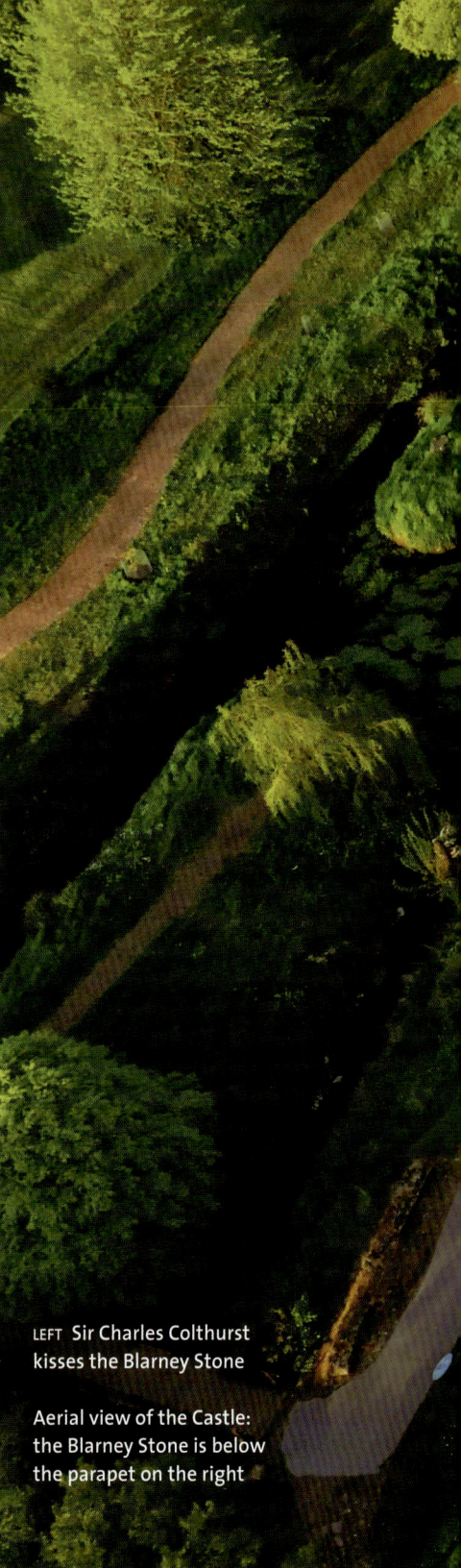

LEFT Sir Charles Colthurst kisses the Blarney Stone

Aerial view of the Castle: the Blarney Stone is below the parapet on the right

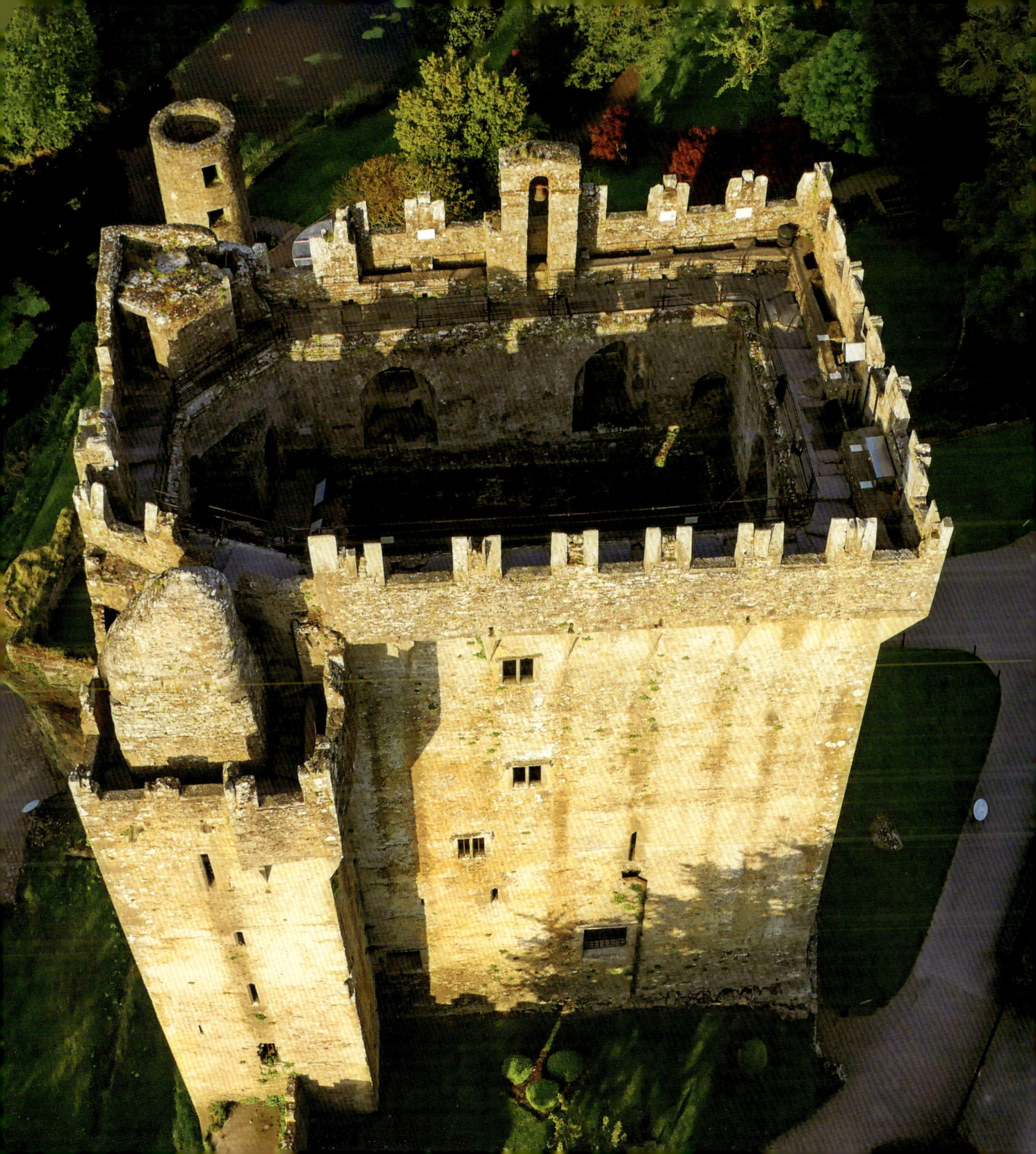

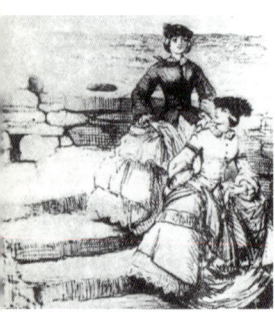

Punch artist John Leitch's drawing of two visitors who have just kissed the Blarney Stone, 1859

RIGHT The Blarney Stone seen from the ground

BELOW Kissing the Blarney Stone c.1900

Another legend is that it was given to the MacCarthy Chieftain by Robert Bruce in thanks for the support that he offered by sending 5,000 kerns (footsoldiers) to Scotland to help him against Edward II, and that it was a part of the Stone of Scone, on which the Kings of Scotland were inaugurated. This custom was practised by Irish chieftains too, and survives today at the coronation of the British monarch, who is crowned on the Stone of Scone.

A further legend tells us that Cormac McTaidhg Láidir MacCarthy, the builder of the earliest part of the Castle, rescued an old woman from drowning in a river. She turned out to be a witch (witches could not cross over water). In gratitude she told him of a certain stone

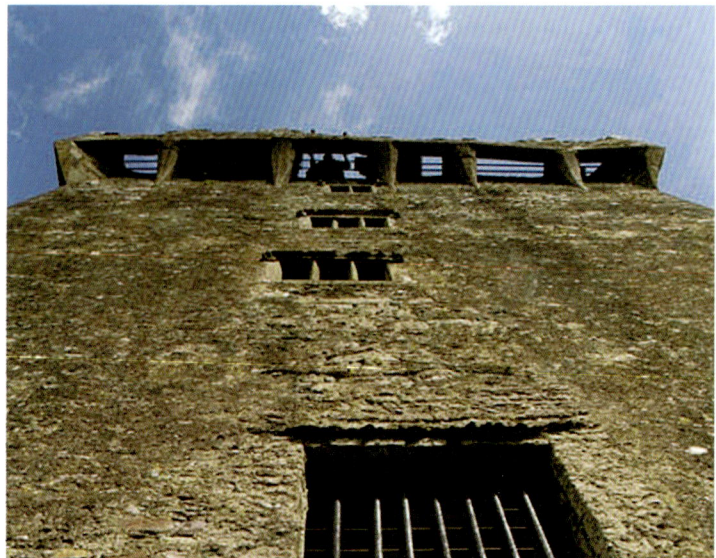

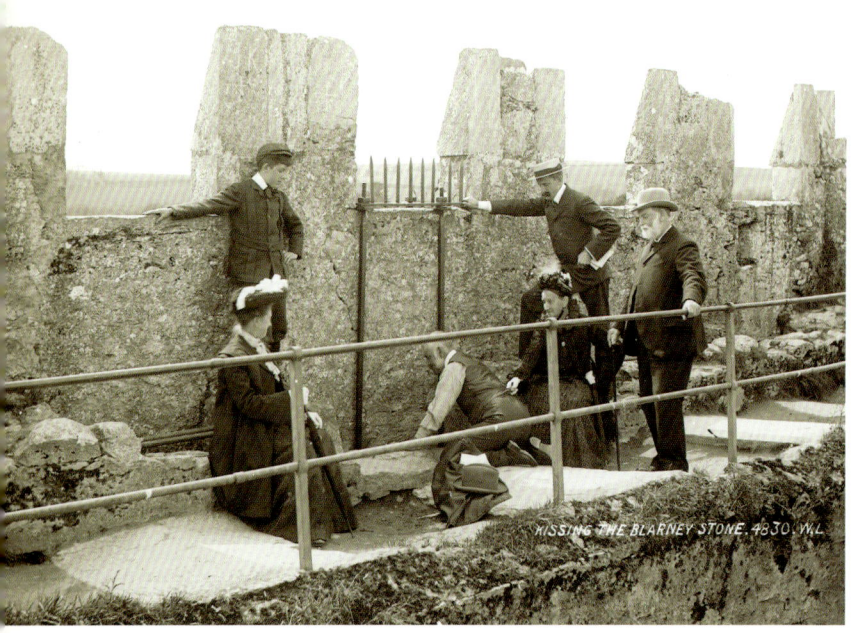

already in his castle that had magic properties and that he could benefit by kissing it.

However, the most elaborate and romantic legend concerns the Queen of the Fairies in south Munster, who was the beautiful daughter of a leading druid. She fell in love with a gallant young chieftain who broke her heart by not returning her love. He was killed in battle and she found his body on a stone on the banks of the river Lee (just south of Blarney). His blood had soaked into the stone. There she grieved, her tears joining his blood in the stone which she continually kissed. This caused her magical powers to be absorbed by the stone itself.

A further version of the legend tells us that Cormac Láidir MacCarthy, being troubled by some intransigent problem, was advised by the Queen of the Fairies that this stone, on which she had wept, had been built into his castle and that if he kissed it his difficulties would be resolved. And so it was. Cormac therefore had the stone taken to the top of Blarney Castle, where it is to be found today.

Whatever its origins, the powers of the Blarney Stone – The Stone of Eloquence – are unquestioned.

Who has kissed the Blarney Stone?

For over 200 years, world statesmen, literary giants, and legends of the silver screen have joined the millions of pilgrims climbing the steps to kiss the Blarney Stone and gain the gift of eloquence. Among those said to have kissed the Stone are:
Sir Winston Churchill, Jedward, Tara Reid, Stan Laurel (while Oliver Hardy waited for him downstairs), ballerina Alicia Markova, US Presidents Ronald Reagan and William Taft, Sir Walter Scott, Sir Mick Jagger and Katherine Jenkins.

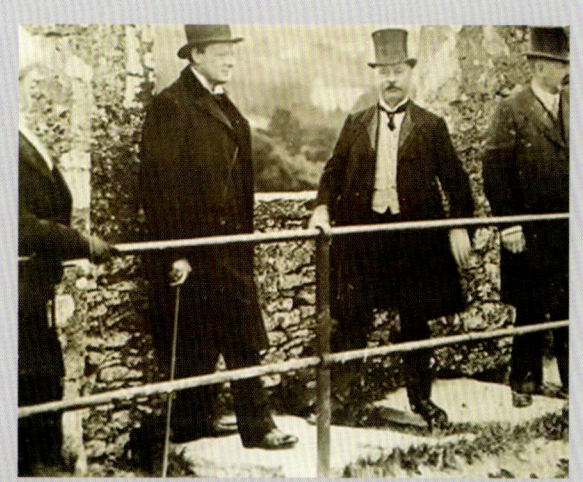

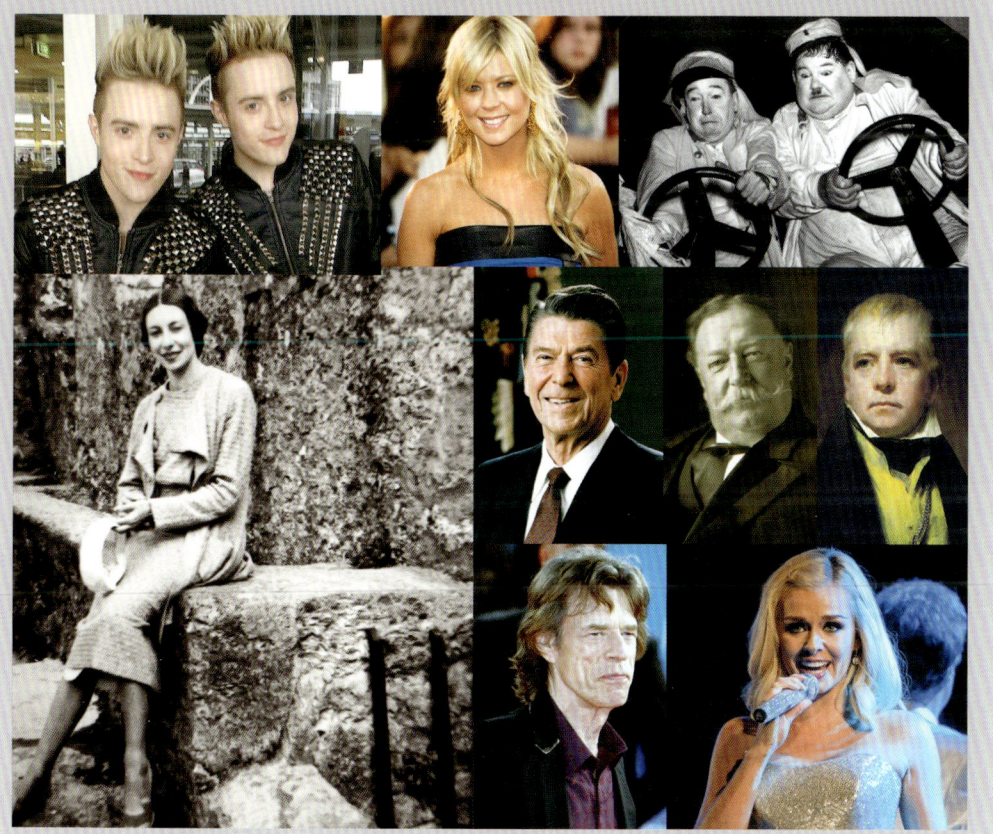

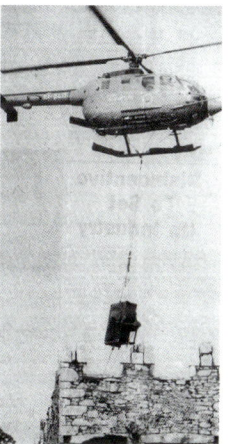

A piano was lifted to the parapet by helicopter for a session by the Cork City Jazz band to kick off the Guinness Jazz Festival in the 1980s by serenading the Blarney Stone

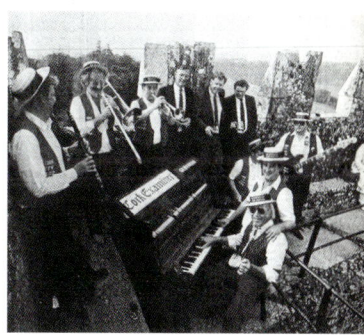

19

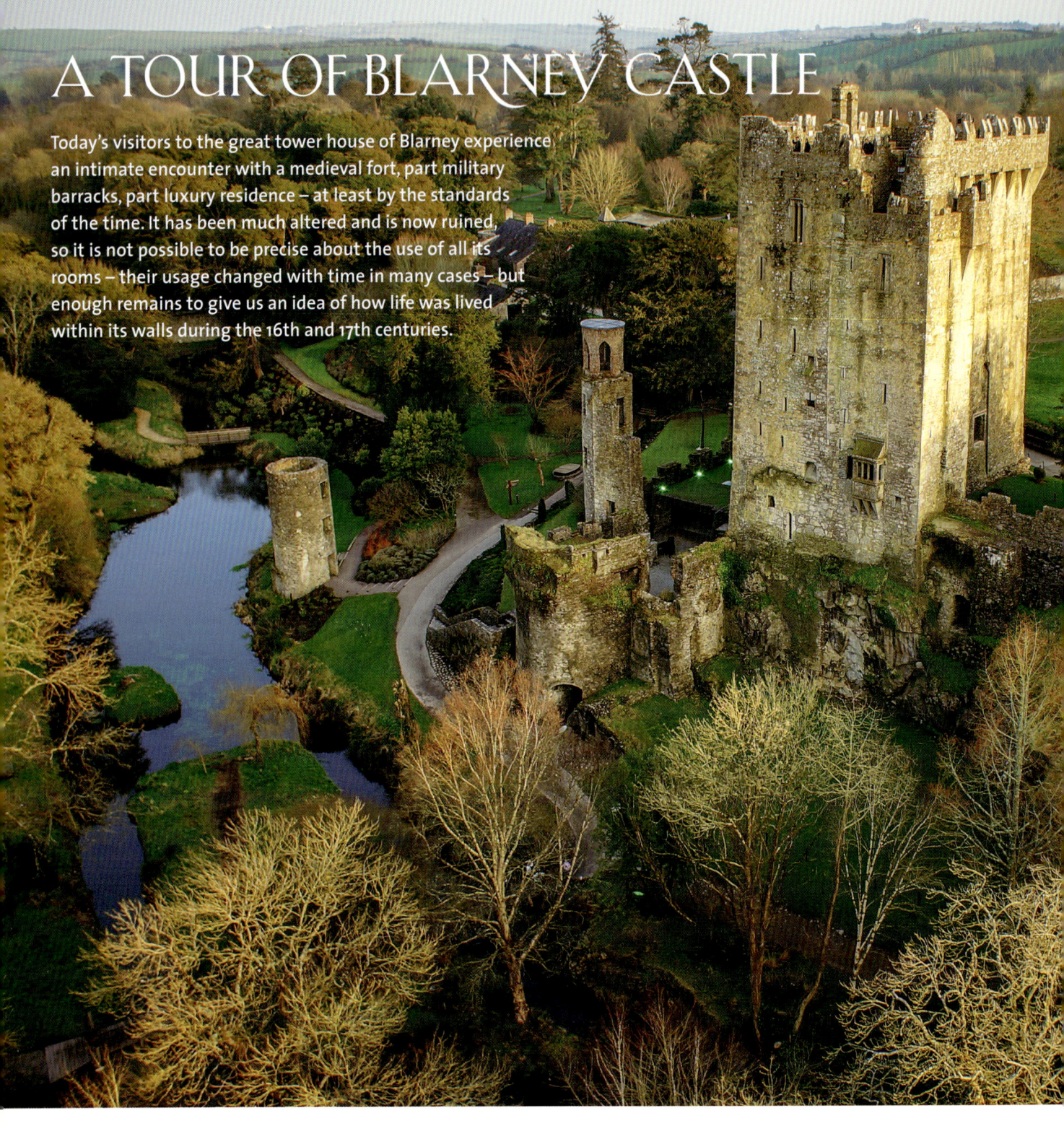

A TOUR OF BLARNEY CASTLE

Today's visitors to the great tower house of Blarney experience an intimate encounter with a medieval fort, part military barracks, part luxury residence – at least by the standards of the time. It has been much altered and is now ruined, so it is not possible to be precise about the use of all its rooms – their usage changed with time in many cases – but enough remains to give us an idea of how life was lived within its walls during the 16th and 17th centuries.

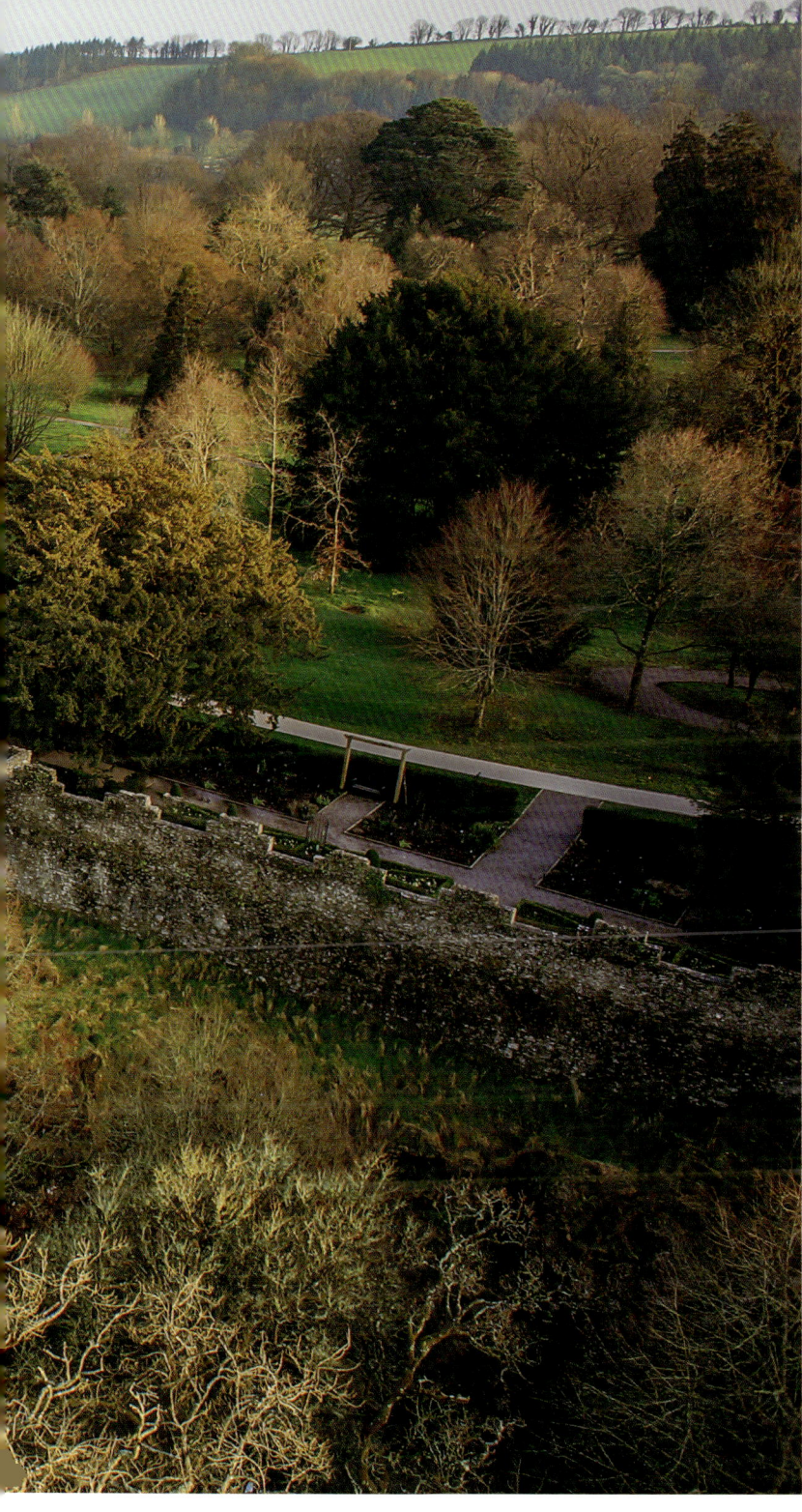

The oldest part of Blarney Castle was probably built around 1480 as one of the strongholds of the McCarthy clan. The Castle is a tower house, a type of fortification built by Gaelic lords and the Anglo-Irish between the 15th and 17th centuries. Tower houses are typically four or five storeys tall with one or two main chambers, plus a number of ancillary chambers on each floor. This type of castle usually has at least one stone vaulted ceiling. The vault was important because not only did it make the thin tower more structurally sound by tying the walls together, it also acted as a firebreak. Without the vault, a tower house was just a big chimney: if a fire started on the ground floor, the whole building could be lost. These castles also have several defensive features, including musket-loop window openings, a roof-walk with battlements that soldiers could fire from, and a 'murder hole' over the main entrance, which allowed occupants to drop things on anyone coming in through the door.

Blarney Castle is an unusually large tower house and it comprises at least two towers – the second one was added in the 1500s. You can see the point where the two phases meet as a vertical line in the masonry on the north elevation. The walls are 18 feet thick at the base, gradually sloping inwards as they rise. This makes the building more stable, but would also have helped with defence: when an object was dropped from the top it would bounce off the wall on the way down and fly outwards into the enemy.

The north elevation, showing the join between the old and new towers, and the line of the bawn wall alongside the Poison Garden

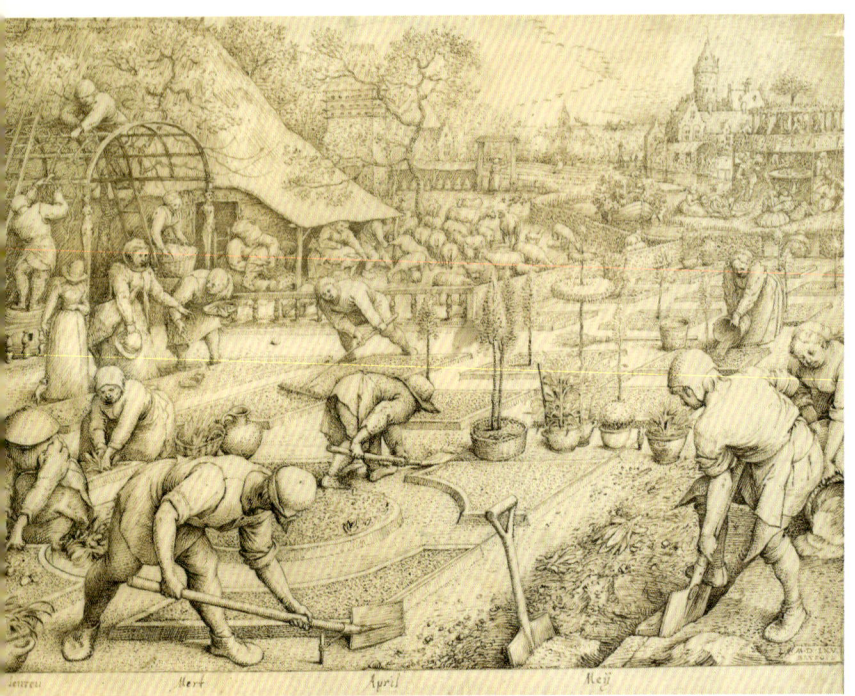

A hive of activity: Pieter Bruegel the Elder's *Spring*, 1565

The walls and bawn

The Castle was originally covered in plaster and whitewashed to protect it against rain and damp, so it would have looked startling, particularly in sunshine. It would also have been surrounded by a defensive wall, which enclosed an area of about 8 acres called the 'bawn'. This sheltered both livestock and people in times of danger, but it was always a hive of activity. Here were to be found blacksmiths, tanners, masons, woodcutters, carpenters, livestock-keepers, horses, cows, pigs and poultry, butchers, cooks, gardeners and all manner of attendants. These included the hereditary protectors of the MacCarthys' property, the MacSweeneys at the gate. The place was full of people, animals, noise and smell. Through all this activity came deputations, traders, messengers and invited guests, often including warriors, learned men, poets and musicians.

The bawn wall is long gone today, but its line is followed by the stone wall along the Poison Garden.

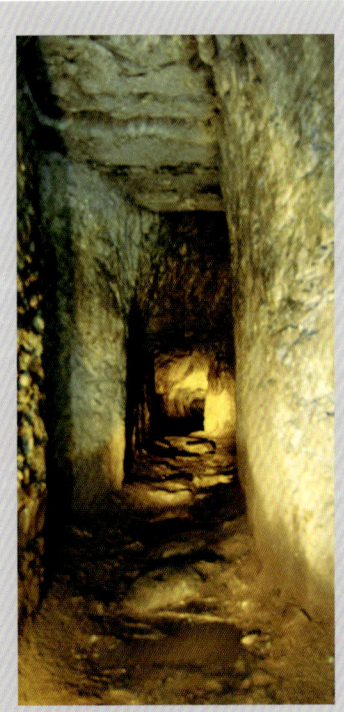

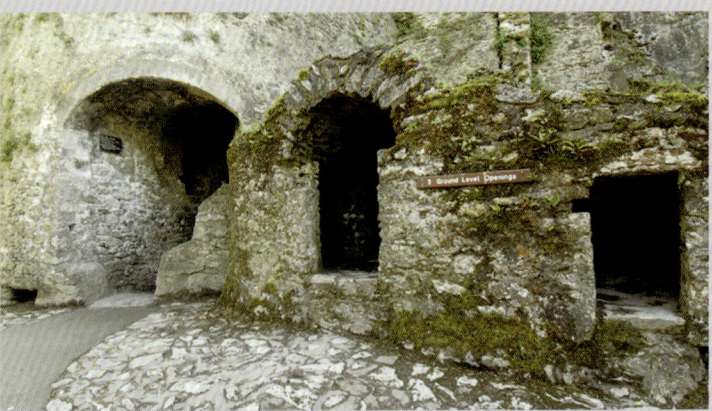

The dungeon

Below the lookout tower on the way up to the Castle are a dog kennel and sentry box guarding the entrance. A third opening in the rock leads to the dungeon – though we do not know whether prisoners were kept here. What is certain is that this contained the Castle well, which had to be protected but kept accessible even if the tower was under siege. This is also the entrance to a labyrinth of hidden underground passages and chambers, now inaccessible to even the most intrepid explorer…

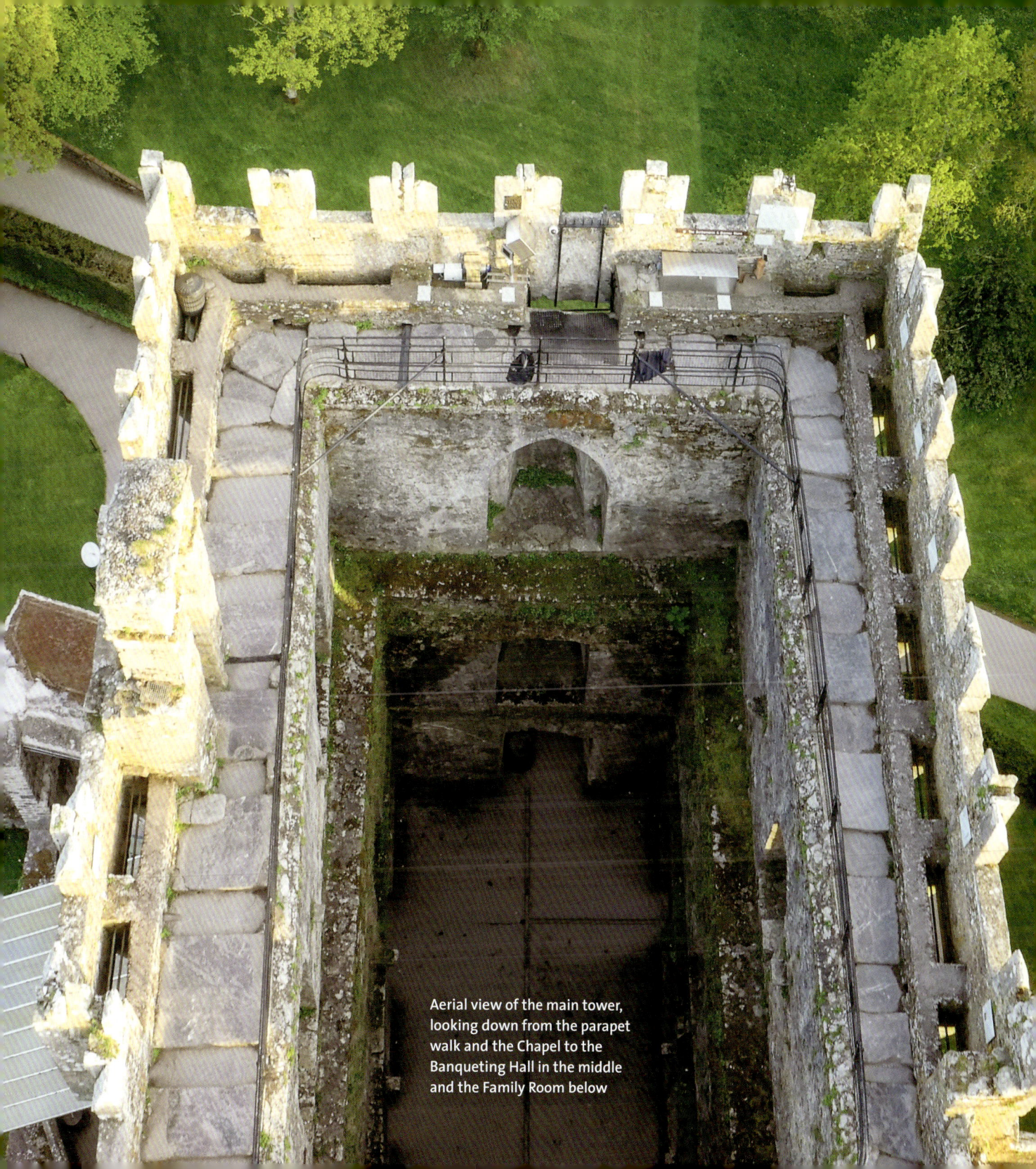

Aerial view of the main tower, looking down from the parapet walk and the Chapel to the Banqueting Hall in the middle and the Family Room below

Entering the Castle

Had we come to storm the Castle and had got as far as the gate, we would face multiple difficulties. Already under attack from the battlements and many musket loops, we would find the entrance facing the cliff's edge, with no room for a battering ram. The entrance door would be covered by an iron grill (a 'yet'), which opened outward but was secured by a strong chain from the inside through a hole to be seen on the left.

If we managed to break down the door, with its awkward yet, we would find ourselves in a confined space with a door in each wall and a 'murder hole' in the ceiling, through which deadly missiles or boiling liquid could be dropped on our heads. The door on the left leads to a store or amoury and had no access to the rest of the Castle. The door on our right leads to the staircase, but would be jammed shut with a beam of timber wedged into an alcove beside the bottom steps. We would then find that the stairs spiral to the right, giving the defender above the advantage of an unimpeded right hand.

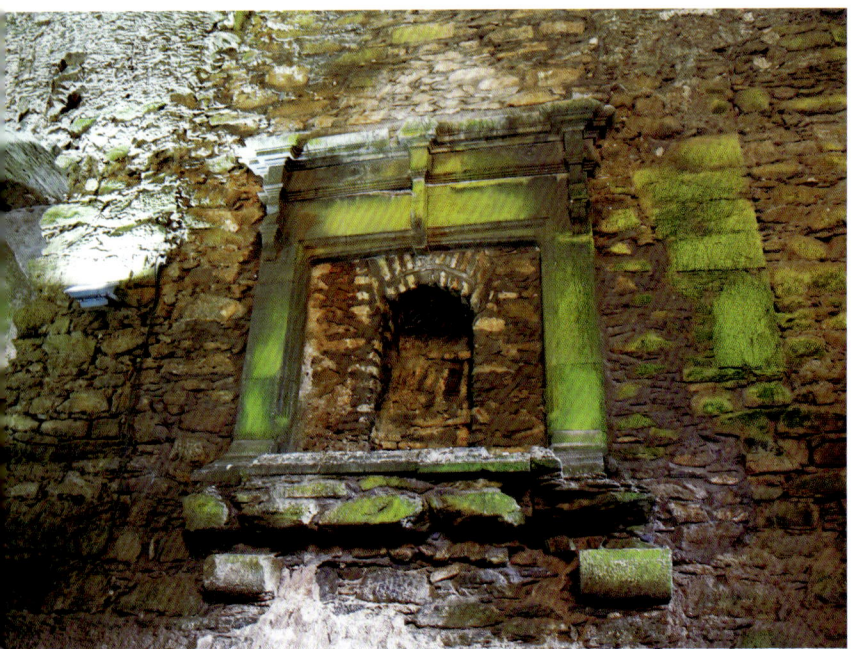

The fireplace in the Great Hall

Today's visitors encounter no such difficulties, but enter the stone-floored storeroom with a narrow door at the far end leading to the guards' quarters. In the MacCarthys' time the floor would have been strewn with rushes on which the men stretched out at night, wrapped in their great cloaks for warmth.

The Great Hall

From the guards' quarters a wooden staircase leads up into a vaulted chamber with a fine 17th-century fireplace. This is known as the 'Great Hall', the nerve-centre of Castle life, where guests were received and entertained. The room would have been sparsely furnished; there were rushes on the floor which the servants changed when important guests were expected. The walls would have been hung with tapestries and portraits, and with rush torches throwing a mellow glow across a game of chess, a lively dance or a conversation over an Irish whiskey.

The smaller rooms

Along a passage in the thickness of the wall is the 'Earl's Bedroom'. This is on the ground floor of the original 15th-century tower house, but its oriel window was added in the early 17th century, giving a grand vista of the Castle's surroundings and the gardens below – and allowing the Earl to look out for possible danger. He would have slept here in a four-poster bed as protection from draughts, but otherwise the room would have been sparsely furnished.

The spiral staircase of the older tower leads up to the 'Young Ladies' Bedroom', with the 'Priest's Room' above it – the floor between them having gone. Nobody knows for certain which 'young ladies' are referred to here, but we do know that the three young daughters of the 14th Lord of Muskerry, Cormac McTeige MaCarthy, were brought up here. The floor was tiled and the walls plastered, and there were wooden benches to dream awhile by the windows or sit by the fire in the corner.

Their good behaviour would be assured if the traditional definition of the room above is correct.

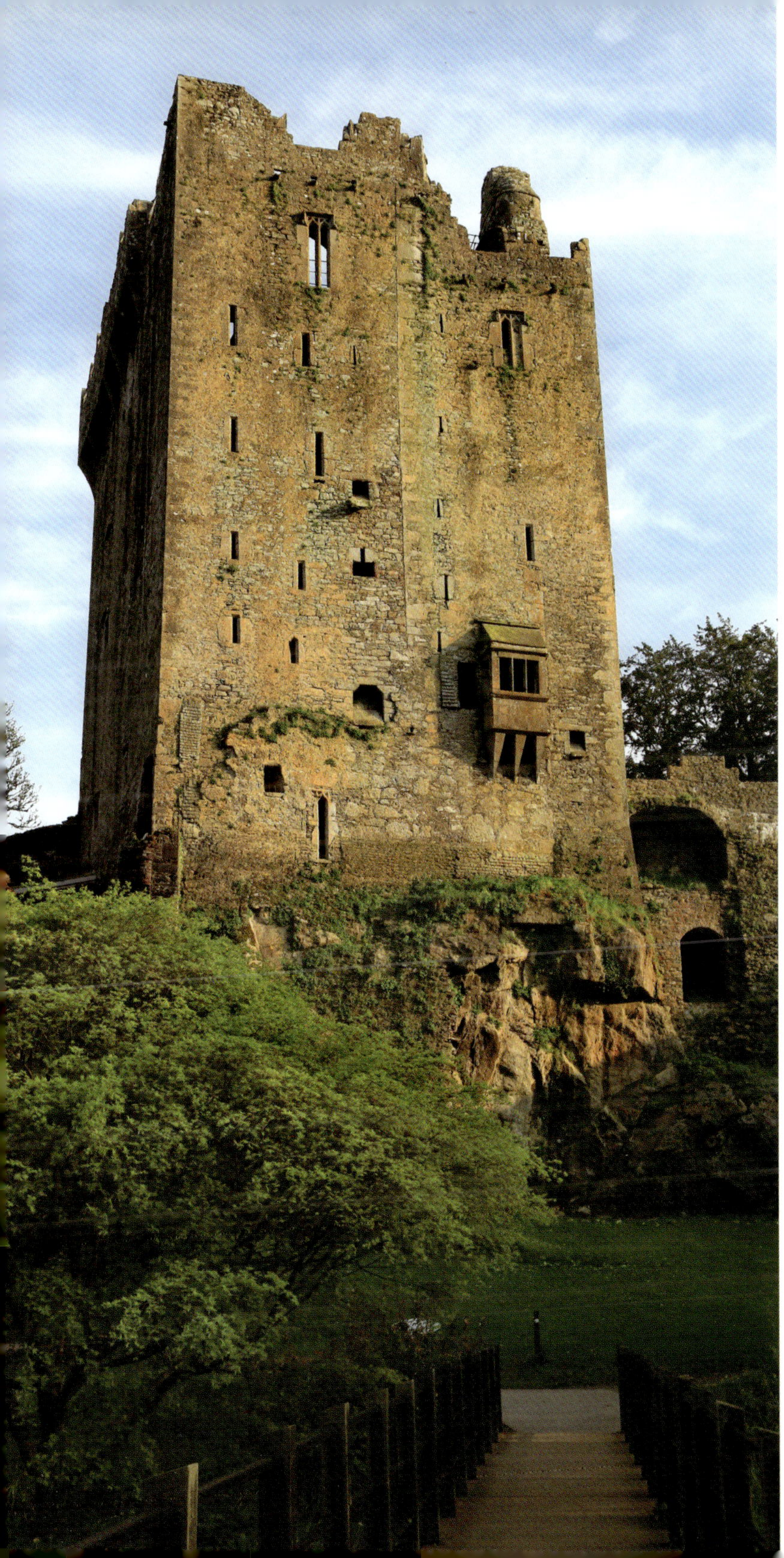

The north elevation, where the Earl's Bedroom oriel window and three square garderobe openings can be seen

The Young Ladies' Bedroom with the Priest's Room above it

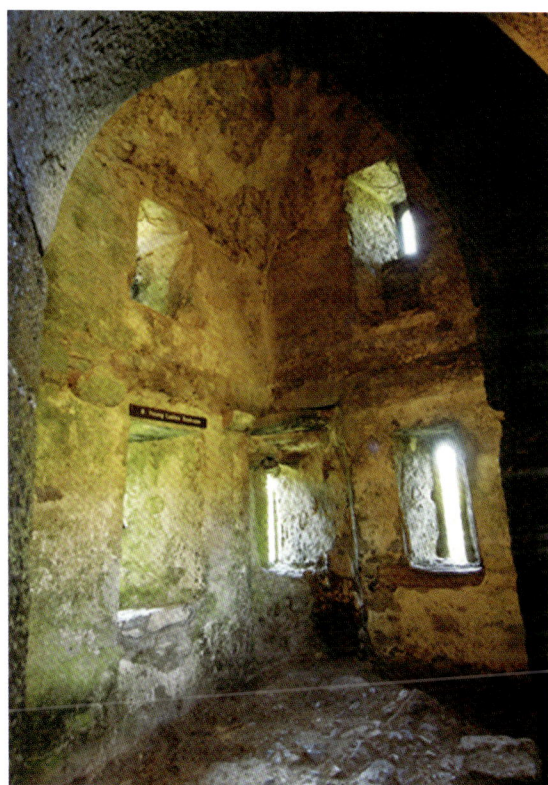

The lack of any gun loops, the space in it west window, perhaps for a small altar, and the shape of the window, suggest its more holy status. This room may even have served as a small chapel.

A further doorway off the same staircase leads to one of the Castle's luxuries: a garderobe or indoor lavatory. A wooden seat for three people would have run along the outer wall. It was built into the north wall – the prevailing wind being from the opposite direction – and a channel above the door led to the south wall, for ventilation. The fact that there are three garderobes in the north end of the Castle suggests that a large household once lived here.

A 17th-century guest

Luke Gernon's *Discourse of Ireland* (1620) describes what it must have been like to be a guest at Blarney Castle. You would be met by the lady of the house 'with her trayne … Salutations paste you should be presented with all the drinkes in the house' – beer, sacke and old ale – 'you must not refuse it'. Then you would be brought to the principal room at the top of the tower, where 'The fyre is prepared in the middle of the hall'; whilst waiting for supper, 'you will not want sacke and tobacco' – meaning that there would be plenty of both. When supper is served, 'the table is spread and plentifully furnished with variety of meates, but ill cooked and without sauce … They feast together with great jollity and healths around; towards the middle of the supper, the harper begins to tune and singht irish rhymes of auncient making.' The bedding arrangements we too might find strange. Gernon comments: 'if the company be greate, you may happen to be bodkin in the middle.'

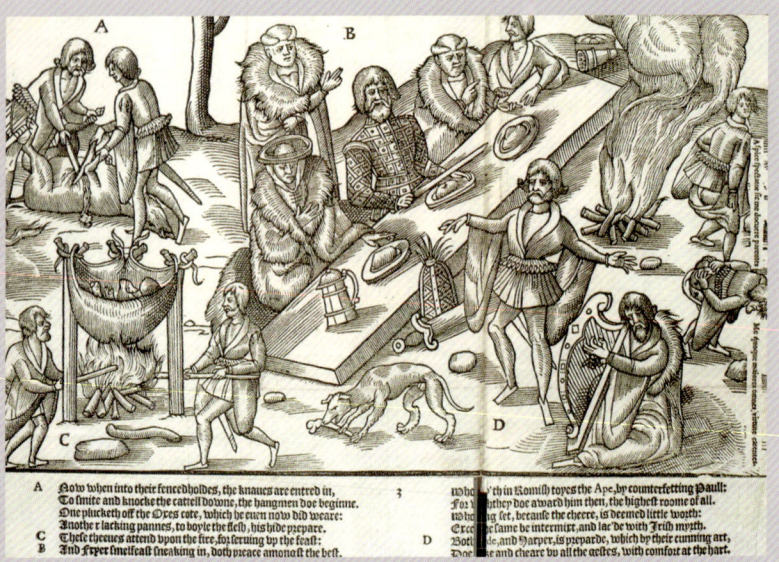

An Irish banquet from John Derrick's *Image of Irelande*, 1581

The kitchen and battlements

The room above the 'Priests's Room', perhaps once the finest bedroom, was converted in the 16th century into the kitchen. Here it was next to the original Banqueting Hall – and its position high on the top floor reduced the risk of fire and meant that there was a ready supply of boiling oil to pour from the parapet onto unwelcome guests. At one end is a large arch with an enormous chimney above it (now blocked), for roasting a full beast. At right angles to this is a smaller arch with a chimney (also blocked), no doubt for slow cooking.

The final climb is to the very top. From the narrow wall-walk or 'allure', with huge flagstones smoothed by the feet of countless people, the views are spectacular. While preparing to kiss the Blarney Stone, visitors can look down and imagine dropping missiles onto the besiegers far below through the gaps in the machicolations.

The principal rooms

A flight of steps leads down from the parapet to the serving area outside the kitchen, with a view down to the room called the 'Chapel' and the 'Banqueting Hall' beneath it. When the Castle was first built, it is likely that what is now called the 'Chapel' was in fact originally the Banqueting Hall: it is the largest of the principal rooms, occupying the whole floor at this

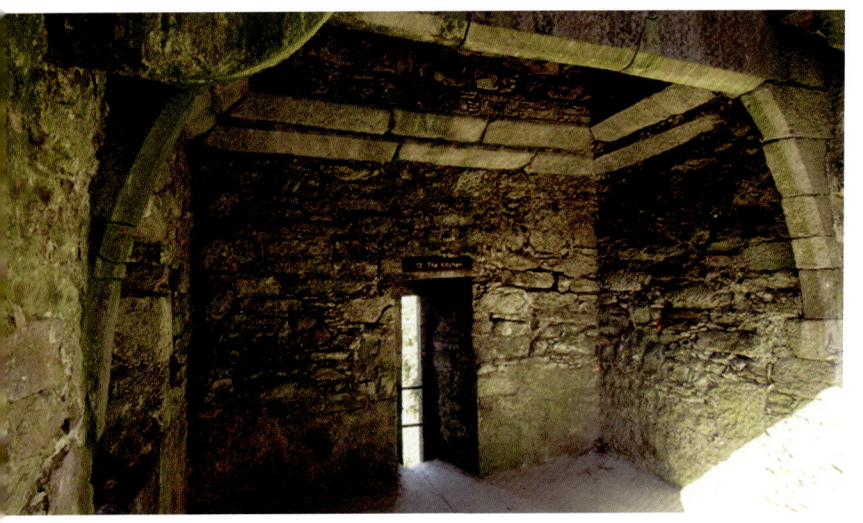

Flat arch on corbels above the huge main fireplace in the kitchen

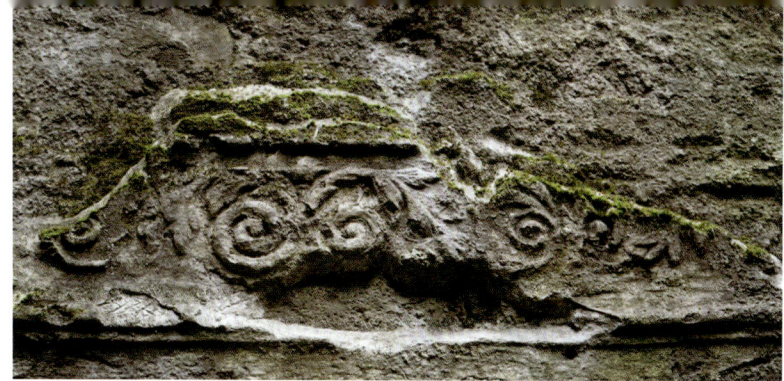

Fragment of 17th-century decorative plasterwork on the wall of the Family Room

level, and has the finest architectural treatment, with pointed arches on three walls. This was where the household gathered for Mass said in Latin, while the chaplain also acted as tutor to the younger members of the family.

The main staircase down to the second floor is wider and easier to use than the one in the older part of the Castle. Explore every passageway and you will find yourself at the wide doorway to the 'Family Room', the main room on this floor, with a view up to the 'Banqueting Hall' or 'Chapel', above. At the north end of the 'Family Room' can be seen the remains of the vaulted ceiling, probably removed when the manor house was added during the first half of the 17th century, which involved major structural alterations to the Castle itself. This was when the fireplace, now blocked, was added on the east wall.

The 'Banqueting Hall' was the heart of the social life of the Castle: feasting was a way of life, combining dinner with a whole night's entertainment. An elaborate series of courses was served, fish, eggs, fowl and roast meat, all highly spiced to keep them fresh. And so a plentiful supply of drink was on hand – mead, beer, wine and whiskey. Seated on his great chair at the head of the long oak table, the Clan Chieftain presided at the banquet. The high ranks sat around him, 'above the salt', the rest sat 'below the salt'. The Castle steward supervised the servants, ensuring that all guests were served with a ceremonial befitting their rank. As the meal progressed, the Chieftain's bard would provide entertainment by playing his harp and singing songs that celebrated the prowess of the MacCarthy Clan.

The fireplace on the north wall of the Family Room below is enormous, flanked with cut stone tablets and a mantle shelf running the full width of the room, very close to where the beams of the ceiling would have been. On the south wall opposite is a rare fragment of early 17th-century plasterwork, the remains of a frieze that would once have decorated the walls of this room. In contrast to the Banqueting Hall, the Family Room was a place for warm gatherings and homely talk around a blazing log fire.

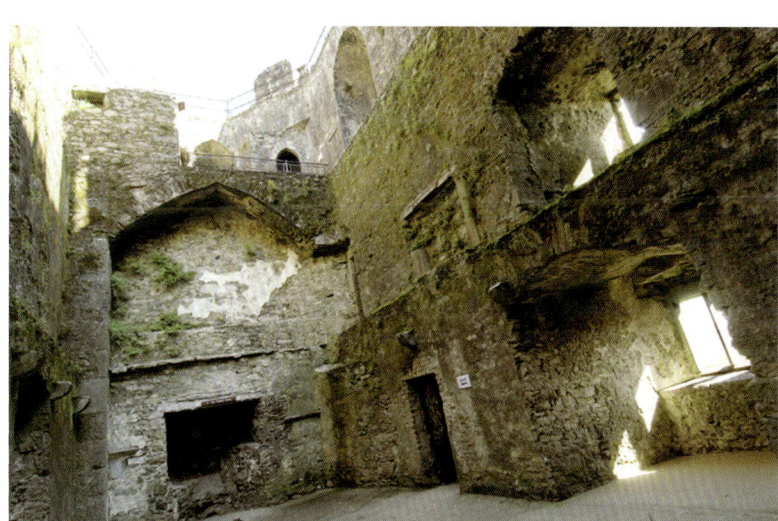

The Banqueting Hall vault above the large Family Room fireplace

BLARNEY HOUSE

Blarney House glimpsed through the trees

OPPOSITE Aerial view of Blarney House with the lake in the background

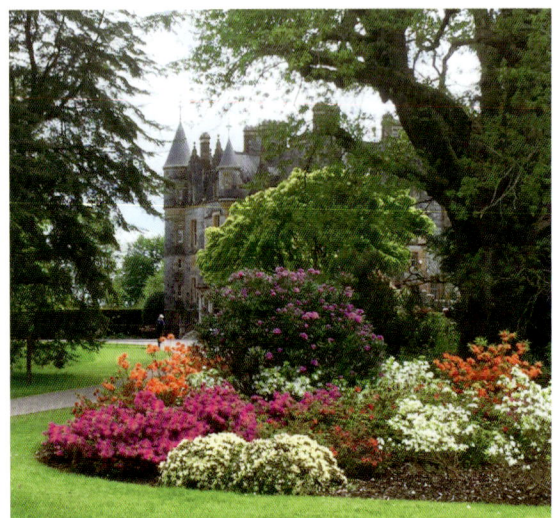

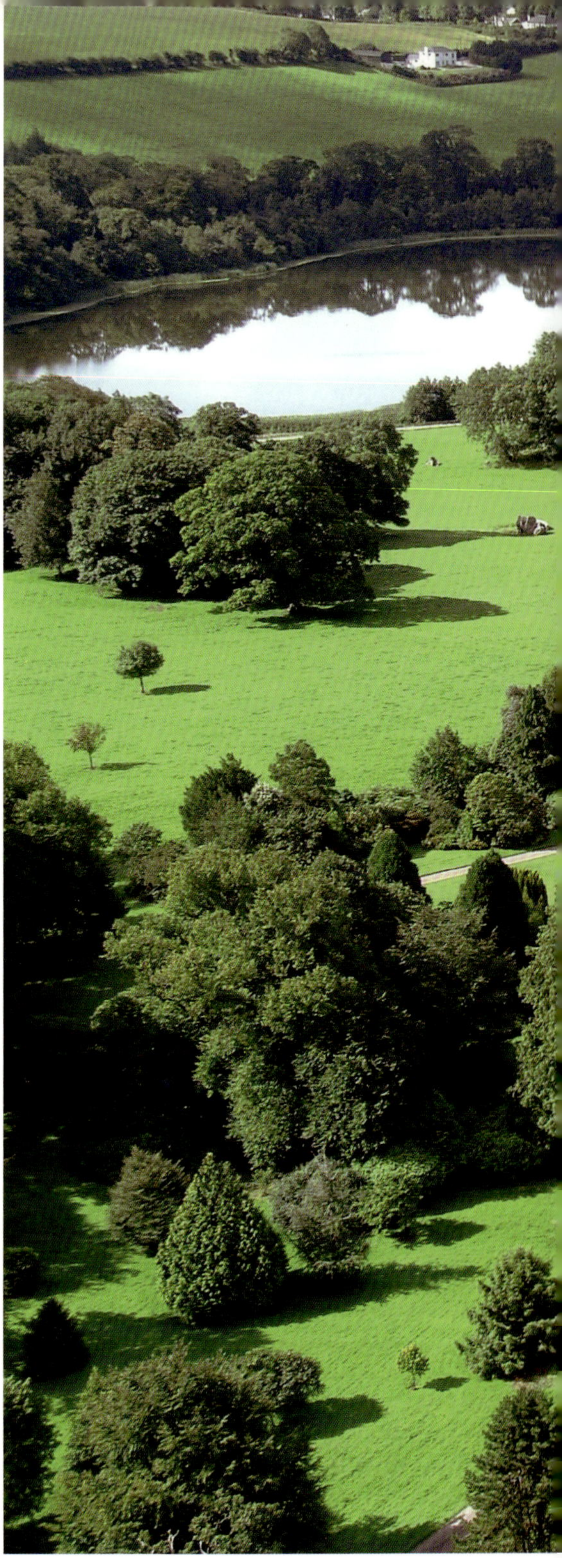

Built in 1874 to welcome the return of the family after an absence on 54 years, Blarney House may surprise by being in the Scots baronial style, which is rare in the southern half of Ireland. Its architect was John Lanyon from Belfast, who had already acted as principal architect for the Marquis of Donegal's Belfast Castle on the slopes of Cave Hill overlooking Belfast City. The two buildings share many features and both are redolent of the romanticism of Sir Walter Scott – who indeed visited the old Castle to kiss the Blarney Stone.

Typical of High Victorian buildings, Blarney House incorporates elements of a number of other styles. Its porch is neoclassical and comes from the Colthursts' house at Ardrum, a neighbouring estate (as do the marble chimneypieces inside). Above this the first-floor window is embellished with Jacobean strapwork, whilst the skyline is pure Scots baronial with stepped gables and a turret. The skyline is wonderfully lively, with conical roofs to the towers surmounted by decorative finials, and tall chimneys

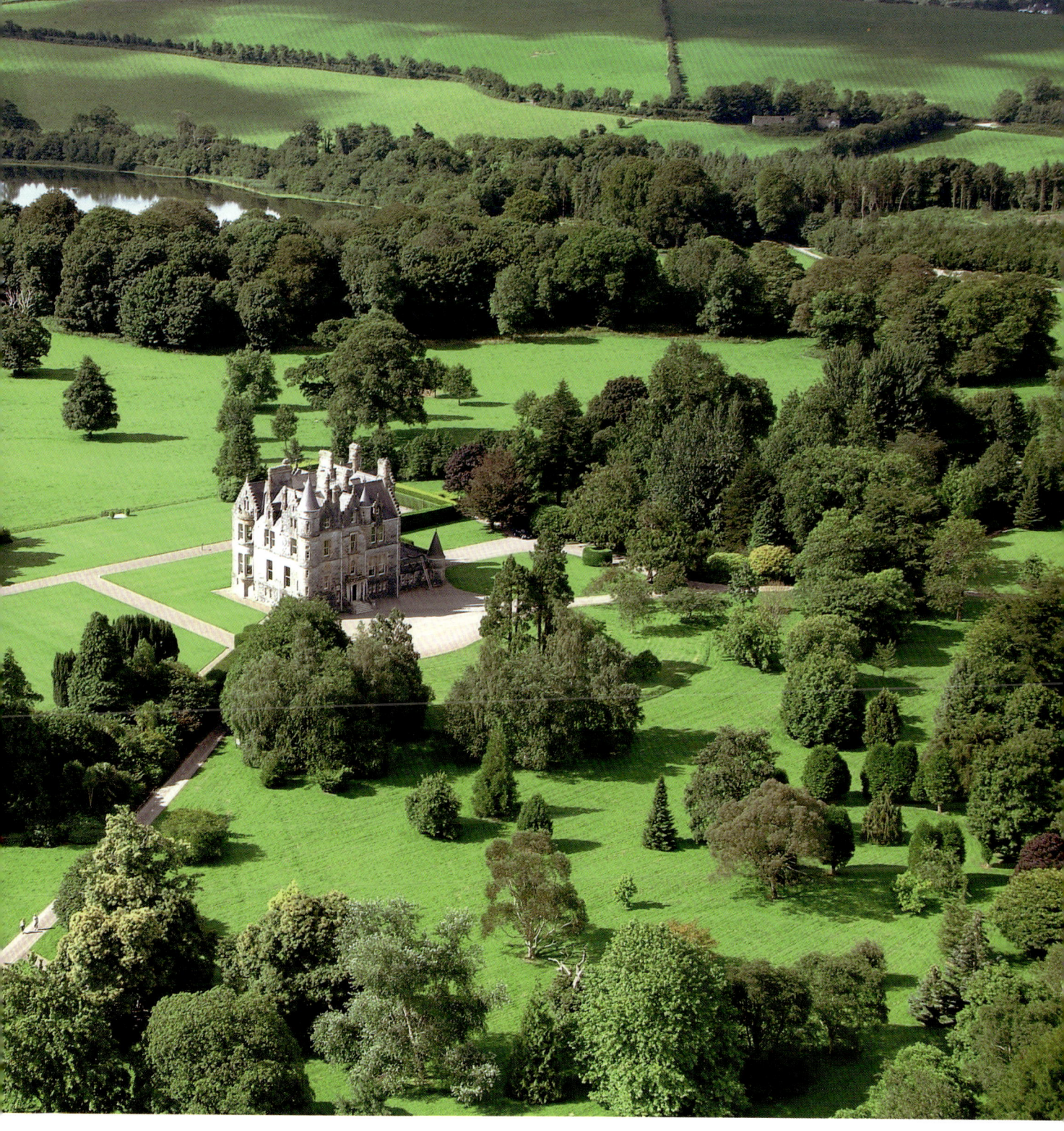

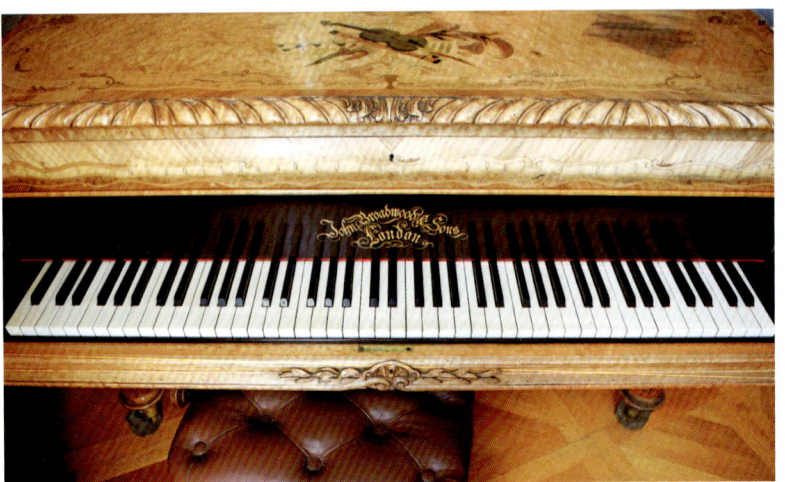

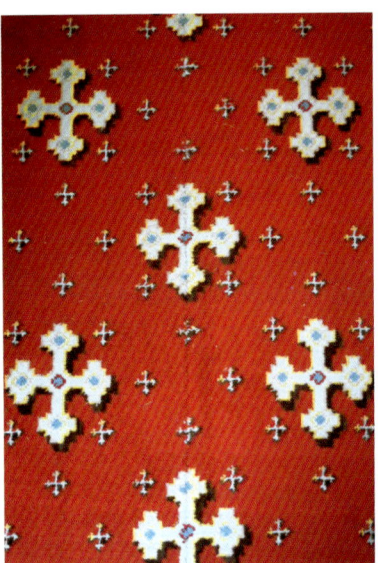

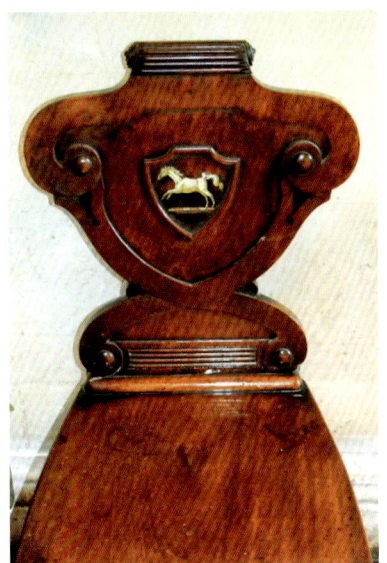

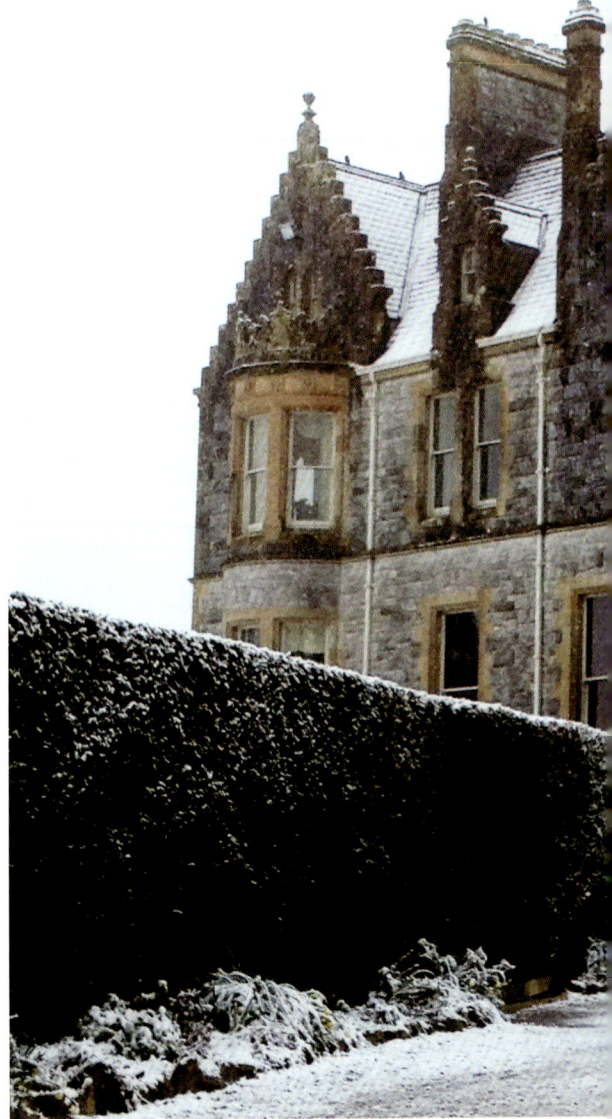

Things to see in Blarney House: the marquetry piano; the Colthurst emblem – a young horse or colt – on the back of a chair; and the cross pattern on the Donegal carpet echoing the design of the door lock

galore. The building's romantic character can best be appreciated by catching glimpses of it through the magnificent trees; romanticism is strengthened by mystery.

The baronial scene continues inside. The visitor entering the lofty hall is confronted by a steep, wide flight of stone steps, which have an almost medieval feel of defence. Double doors at the top open to the staircase hall, which is domestic in feel and welcoming. The imposing Jacobean-style staircase is lit from

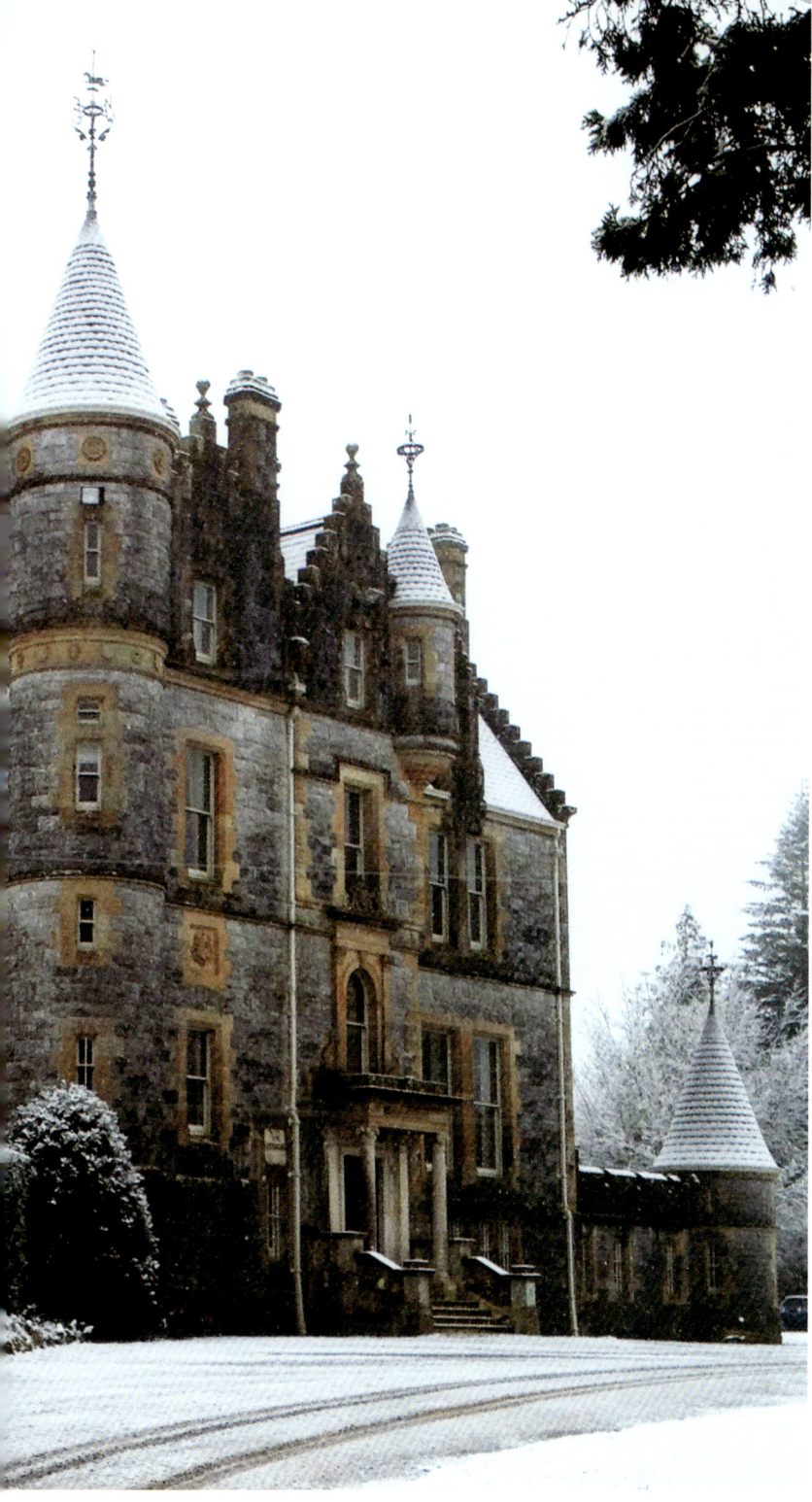

Blarney House in winter

above, and hung with portraits of Jefferyes and Colthurst family members and associates. The staircase rises into a splendid arcade surrounding it on three sides beneath the large skylight.

Whereas the entrance is on the north side and the staircase hall is windowless, the reception rooms are south-facing and flooded with light from large plate-glass windows. Here the decorative style changes to Adamesque. Large overmantel mirrors and splendid chandeliers add to the sense of brightness and gracious domesticity, and the extensive views over lawns, lake, noble trees and grassy hills in the distance all combine to enchant the visitor.

Points of special interest

The uses of some of the rooms have changed over the years. For example, the present library used to be the dining-room, when staff prepared meals in the basement. In the corner turret, diagonally opposite the door from the hall, is the lift which was used for bringing the food from the basement.

Also in the library are stuffed animals displayed in glass cases, much loved by Victorian residents of country houses.

The carved decoration on the fireplaces, brought by the Colthurst family from Ardrum, provide further clues as to original use of the main reception rooms.

The cross pattern on the Donegal carpet in the staircase hall, woven especially for Blarney House, copies the cross design on the inner door lock.

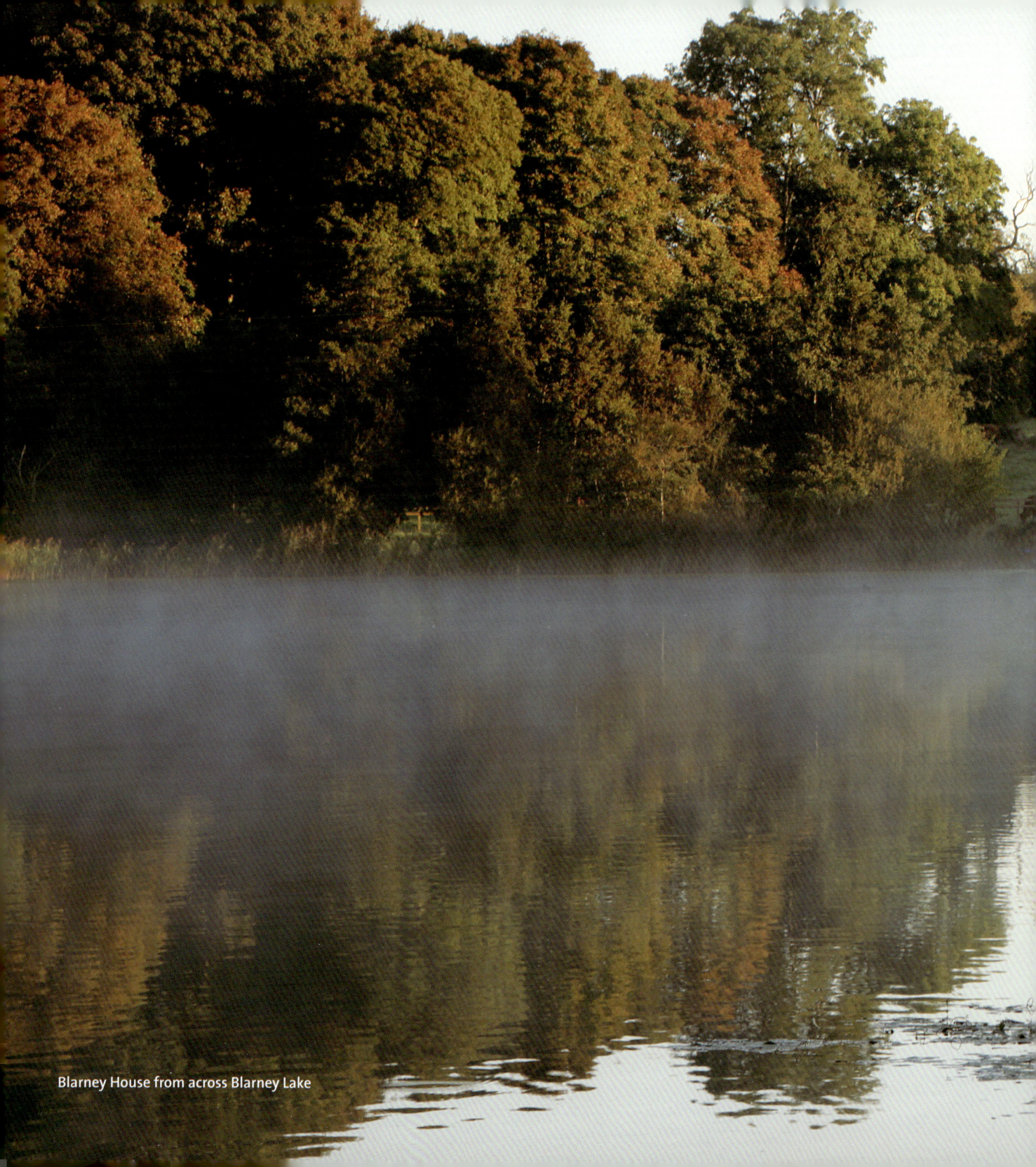

Blarney House from across Blarney Lake

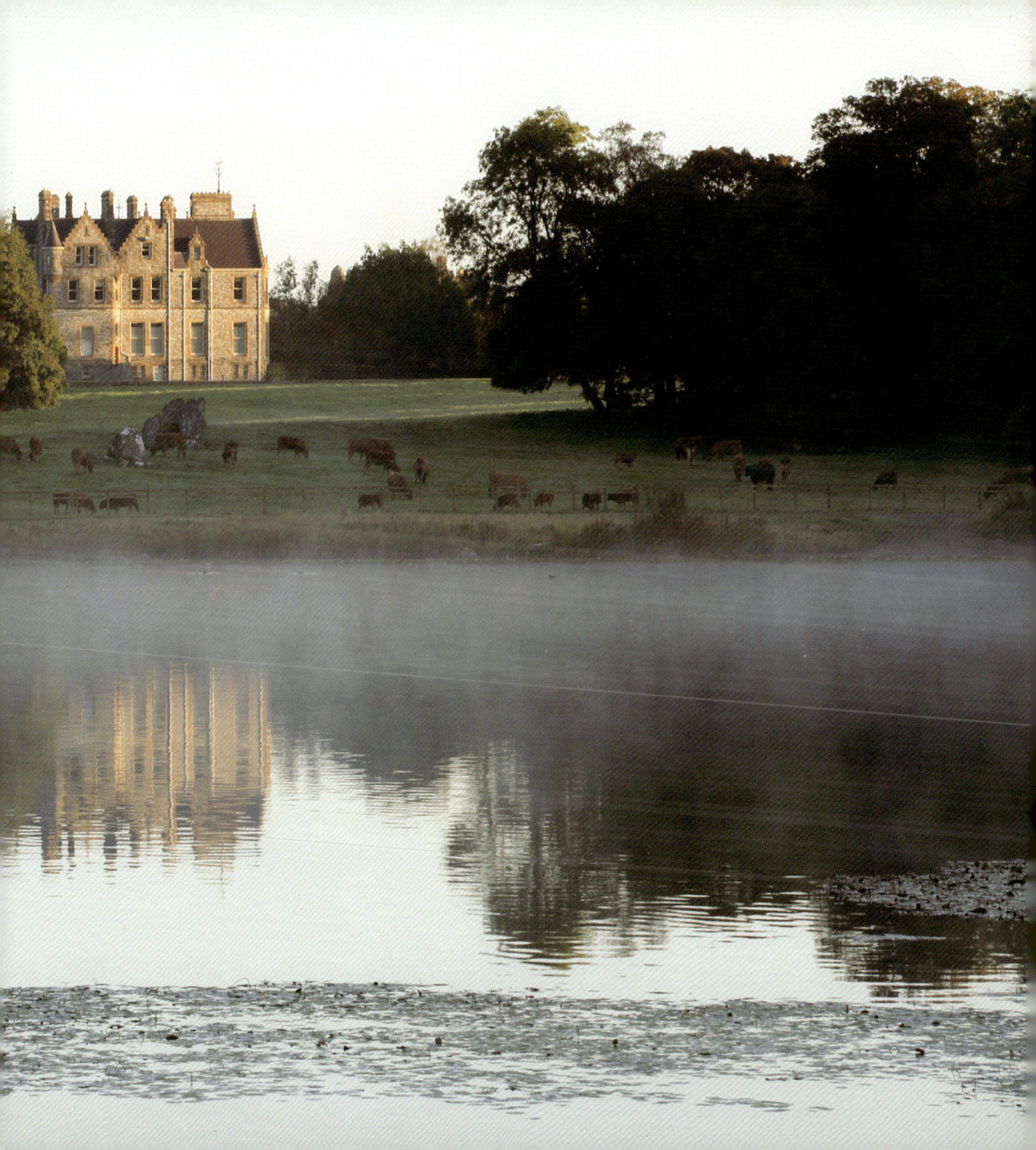

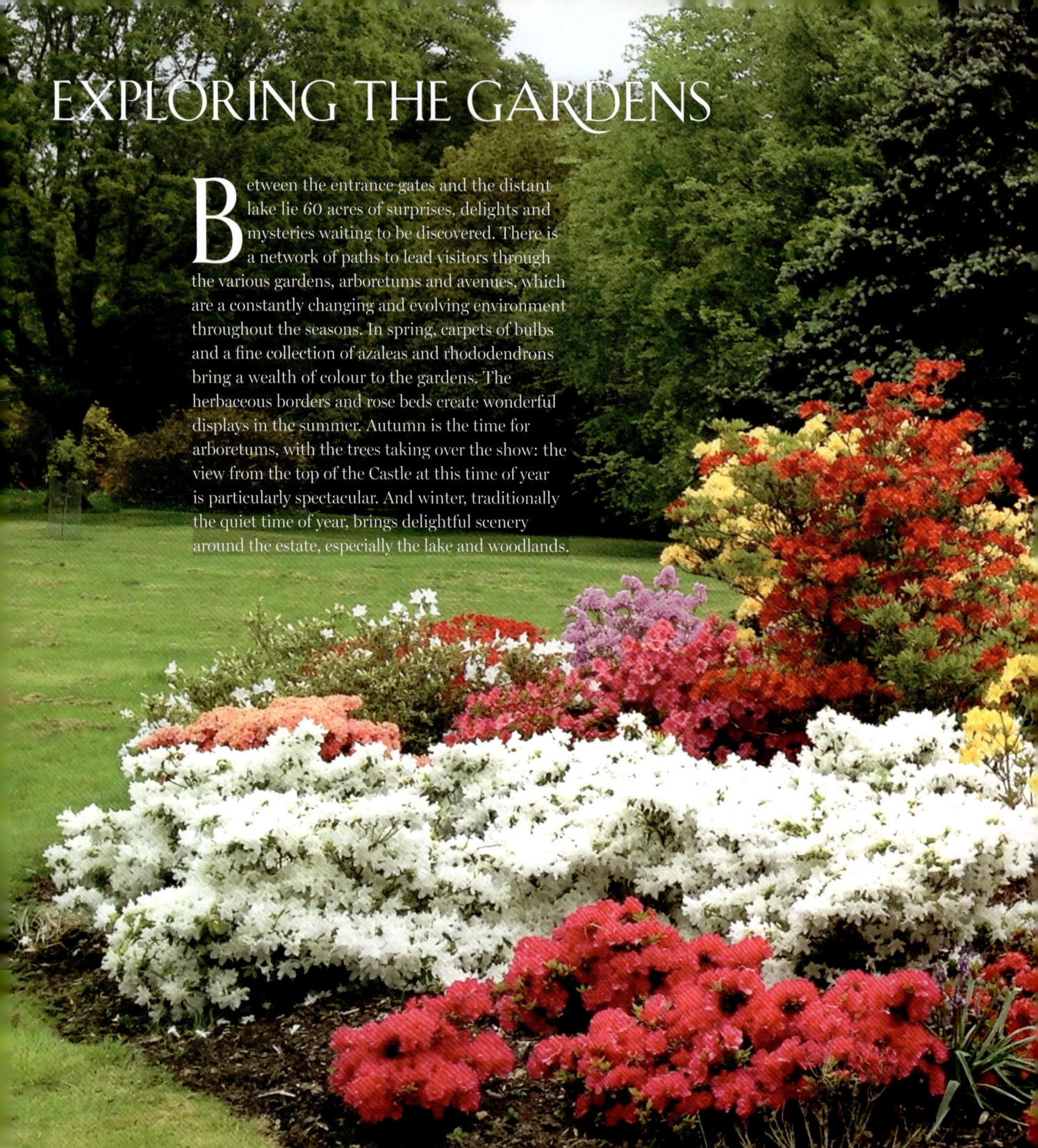

EXPLORING THE GARDENS

Between the entrance gates and the distant lake lie 60 acres of surprises, delights and mysteries waiting to be discovered. There is a network of paths to lead visitors through the various gardens, arboretums and avenues, which are a constantly changing and evolving environment throughout the seasons. In spring, carpets of bulbs and a fine collection of azaleas and rhododendrons bring a wealth of colour to the gardens. The herbaceous borders and rose beds create wonderful displays in the summer. Autumn is the time for arboretums, with the trees taking over the show: the view from the top of the Castle at this time of year is particularly spectacular. And winter, traditionally the quiet time of year, brings delightful scenery around the estate, especially the lake and woodlands.

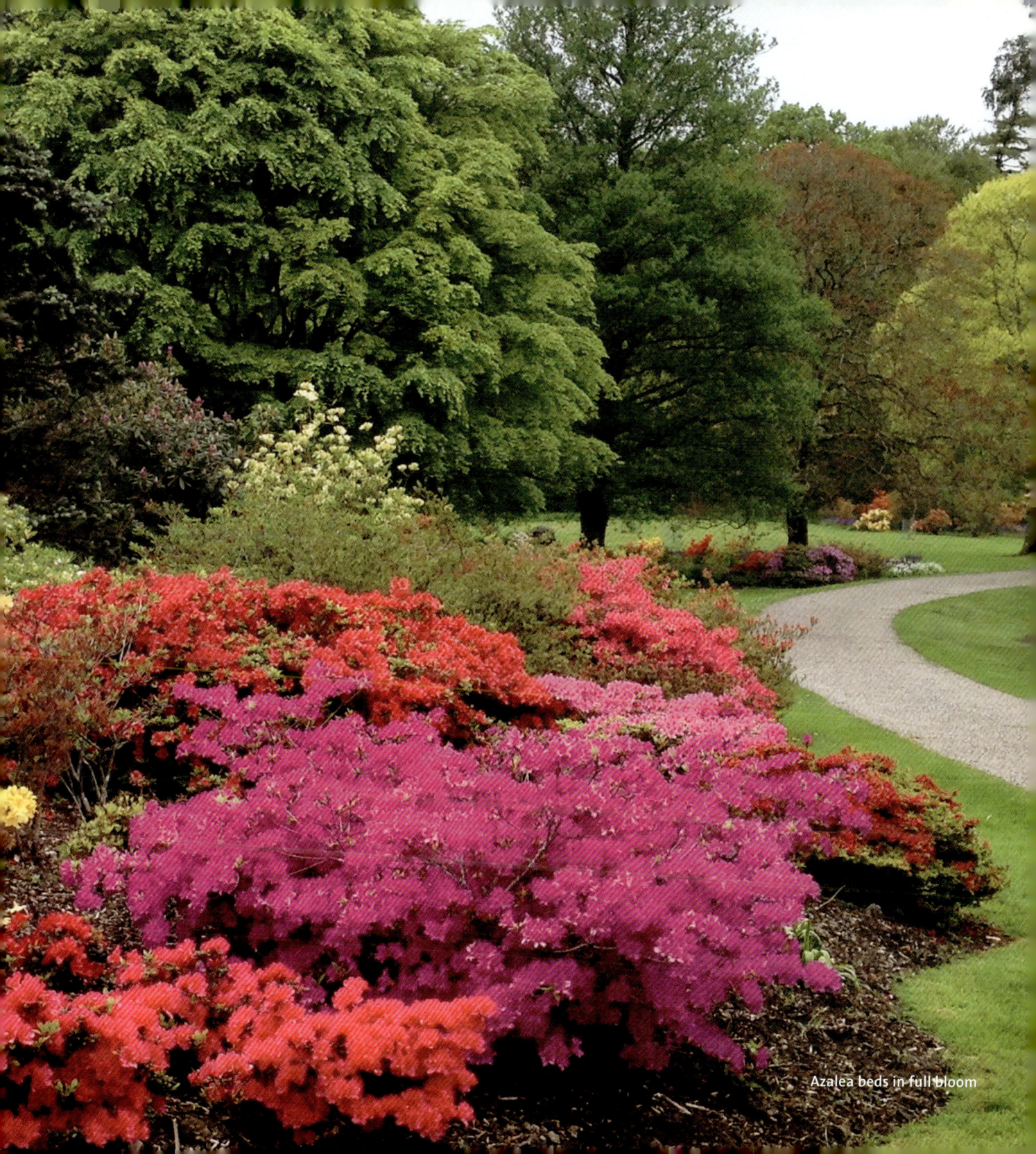
Azalea beds in full bloom

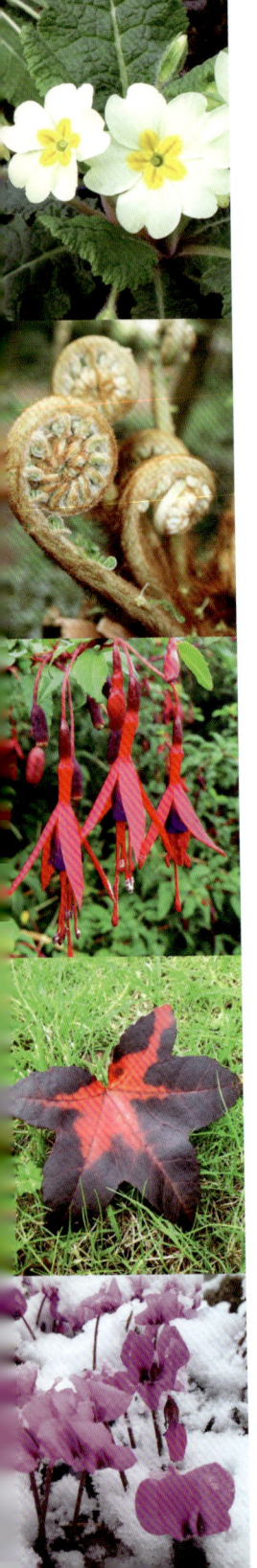

Along the woodland paths you are in the midst of undisturbed nature, the same now as it has been for hundreds of years. Look at the plants around you, from the great trees towering above to the tiniest mosses at your feet.

Another path, leading southwards away from the Poison Garden, passes through camellia bushes, bright with colour in the spring. This leads to a tower in the Stumpery – the only one in Ireland. This garden was created from the roots and branches of bog oak, yew and pine trees, many centuries old, and harbours plants, fungi, insects and grubs which need this particular habitat.

The avenue leading away from Blarney House runs alongside the Belgian Beds, so called because their original plants came from specialist nurseries in Belgium early in the 20th century. In spring their scented azaleas are alive with colour.

The Irish Garden takes the form of a natural woodland walk which contains only native species. This is a place of quiet and the sweet air is softly filtered by the trees all around. Here nature is allowed to do what it does, with minimum interference. Fallen trees are allowed to lie, encouraging all sorts of wildlife; regeneration is natural; foreign species are removed. It is both bursting with life, yet deeply calming.

In the Himalayan Valley to the east of the House, important conservation projects are taking place, saving trees that are endangered in their native lands. Here Vietnamese chestnut trees (*Aesculus wangii*) thrive, having been grown from seed, whilst their habitat in the foothills of the Himalayas is under threat.

Other delights to be discovered are the beehives in the Walled Garden, with a window allowing you to watch the bees working without disturbing them; Blarney Lake, home to many waterfowl; and a wildflower meadow, where native flora and fauna thrive.

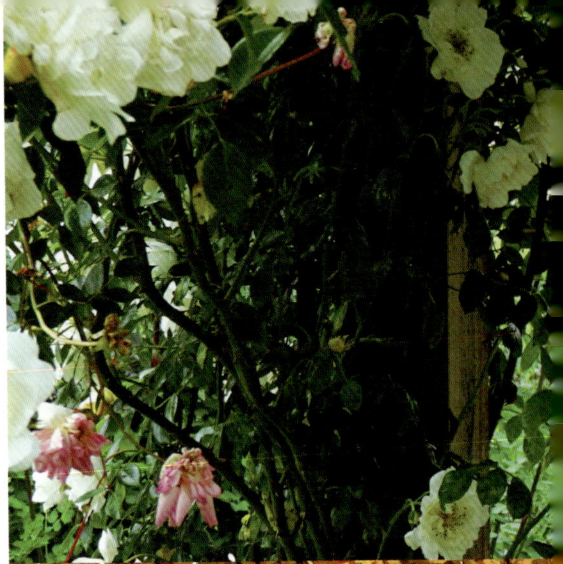

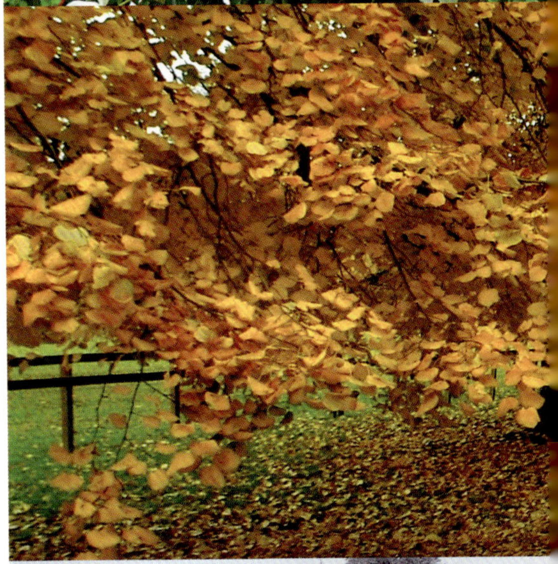

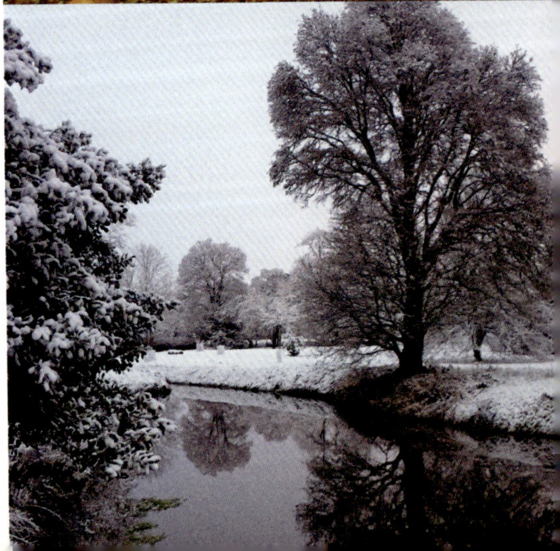

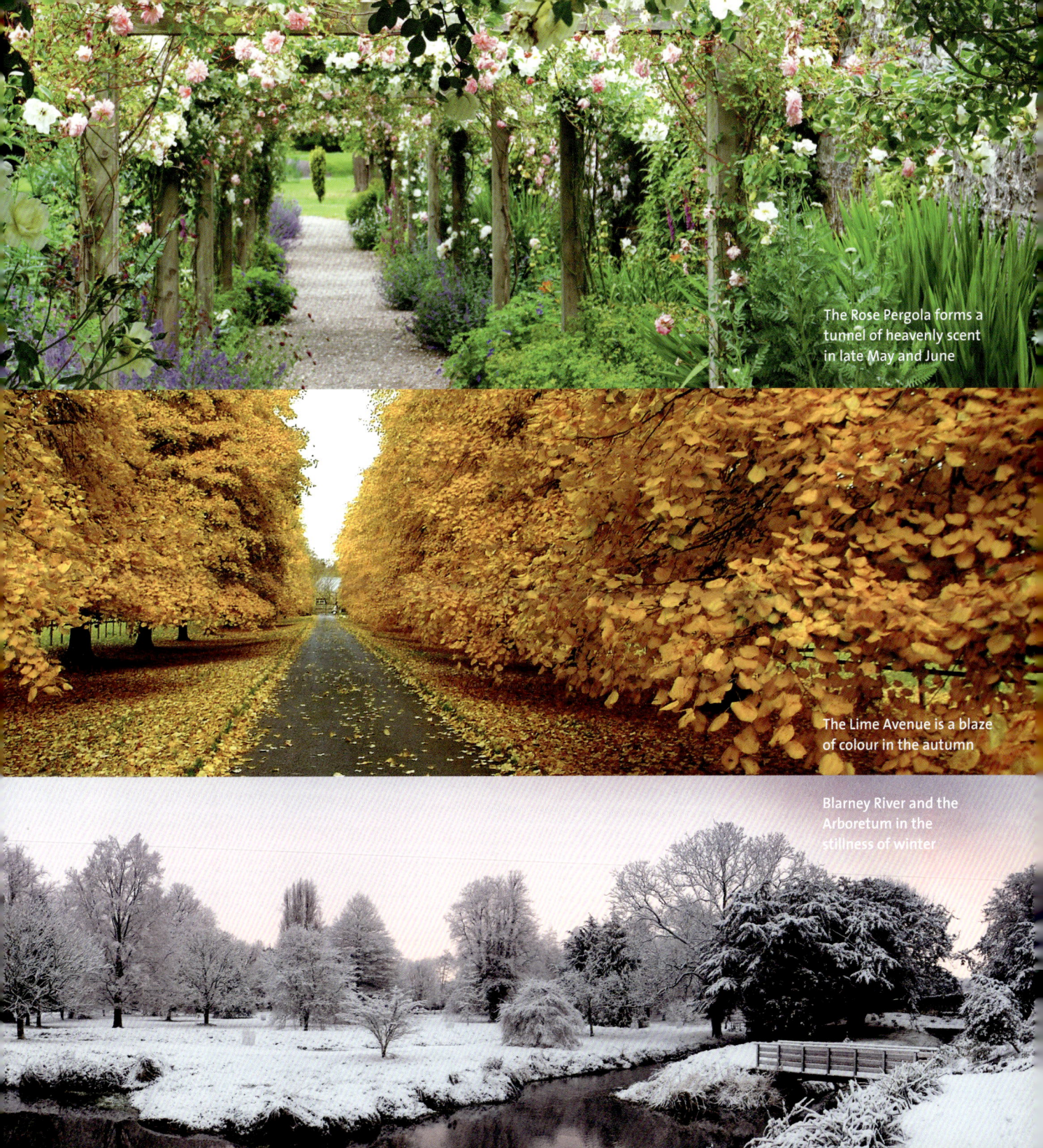

The Rose Pergola forms a tunnel of heavenly scent in late May and June

The Lime Avenue is a blaze of colour in the autumn

Blarney River and the Arboretum in the stillness of winter

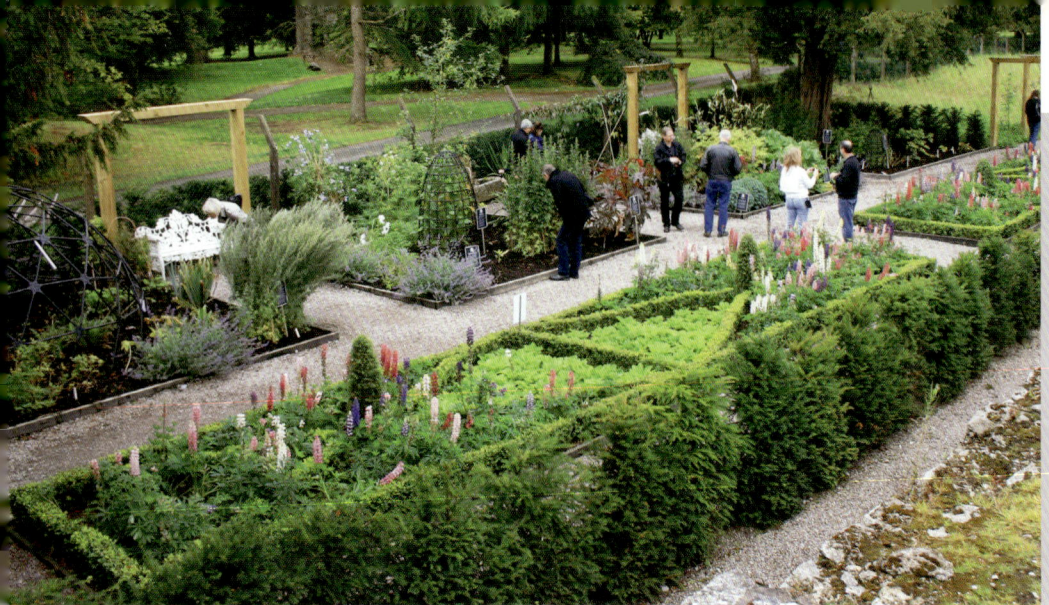

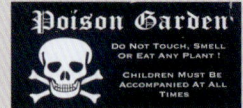

Poison Garden

On the west side of the Castle is the popular Poison Garden – the delight of Blarney's witches! This is laid out by the remaining section of the bawn wall with its 17th-century battlements, and is reminiscent of a 17th-century physic garden in its formal parterre plan. The explicit notices are intriguing and the most dangerous plants are caged...

SPECIALIST GARDENS

Board Walk and Water Garden

The raised board walk, surrounded by *Gunnera manicata* ('giant rhubarb') and water-loving plants growing in profusion. Waterfalls add coolness to the scene.

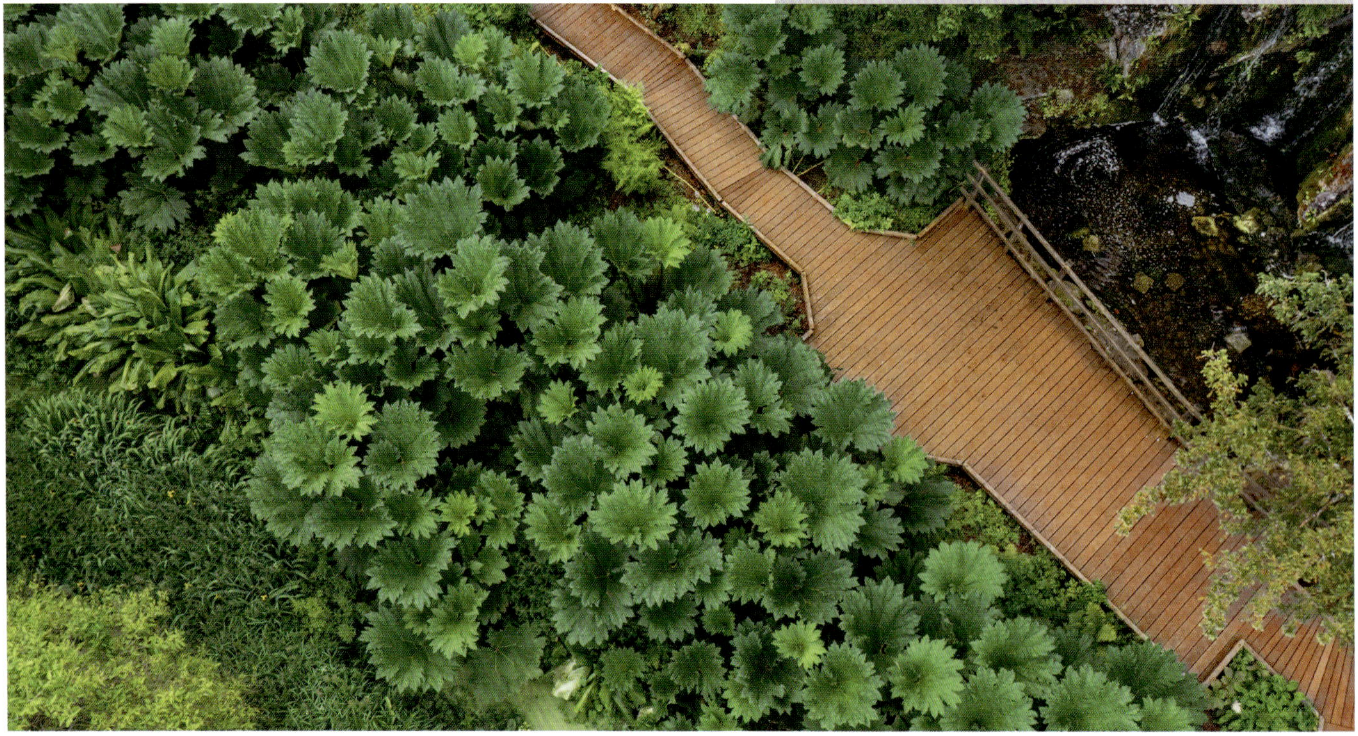

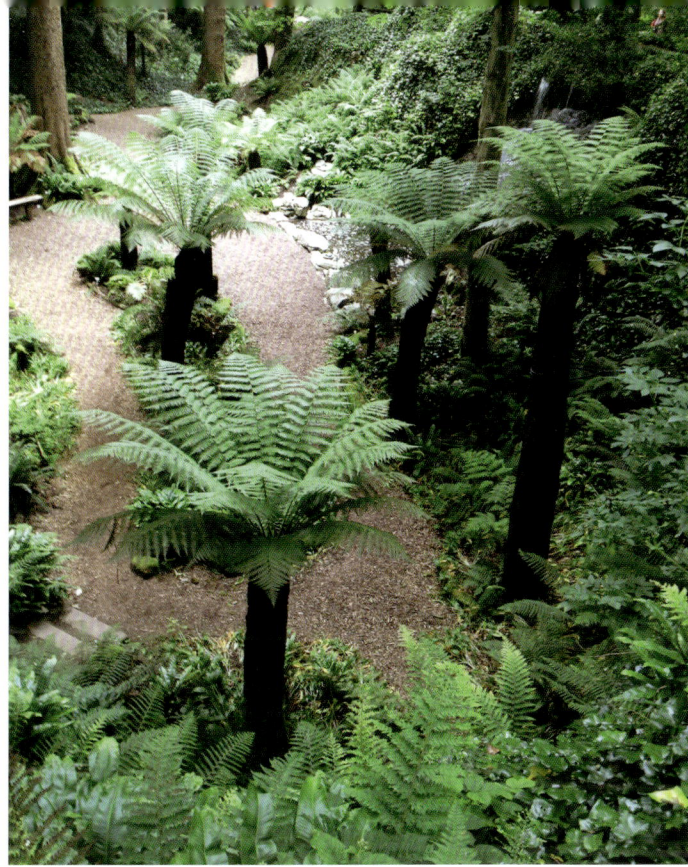

Fern Garden

Across the road from the Irish Garden is an extensive and exotic Fern Garden. The tall Dicksonias (tree ferns) growing here, brought from the other side of the world, are survivors of the Jurassic period. Light is filtered through the immensely high trees and then through the spectacular fronds of the ferns. The place is magnificently still and quiet.

Tropical Border

Banana, yuccas and cordylines provide structure in a border filled with vibrant colours, including the Bird of Paradise plant (*Strelitzia reginae*) and other exotics.

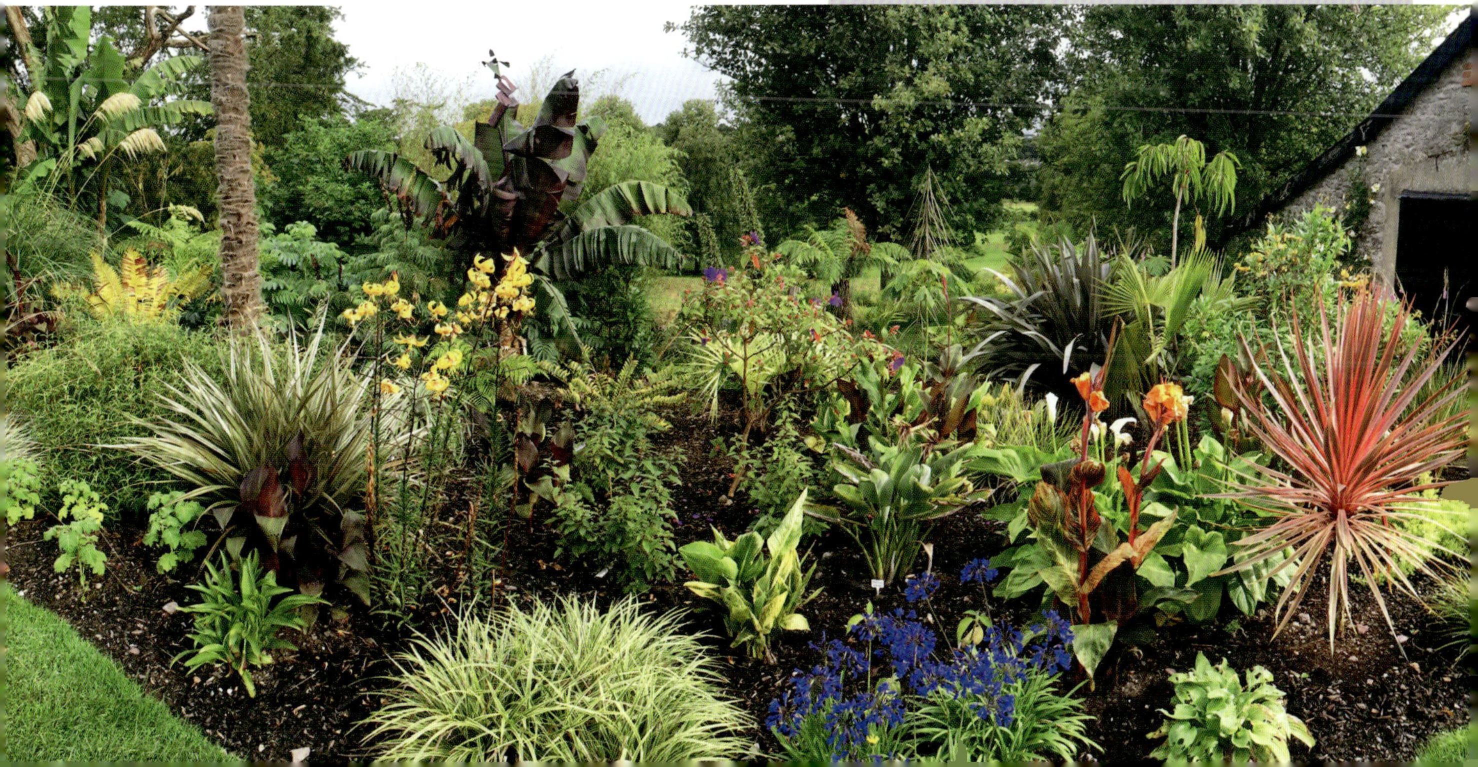

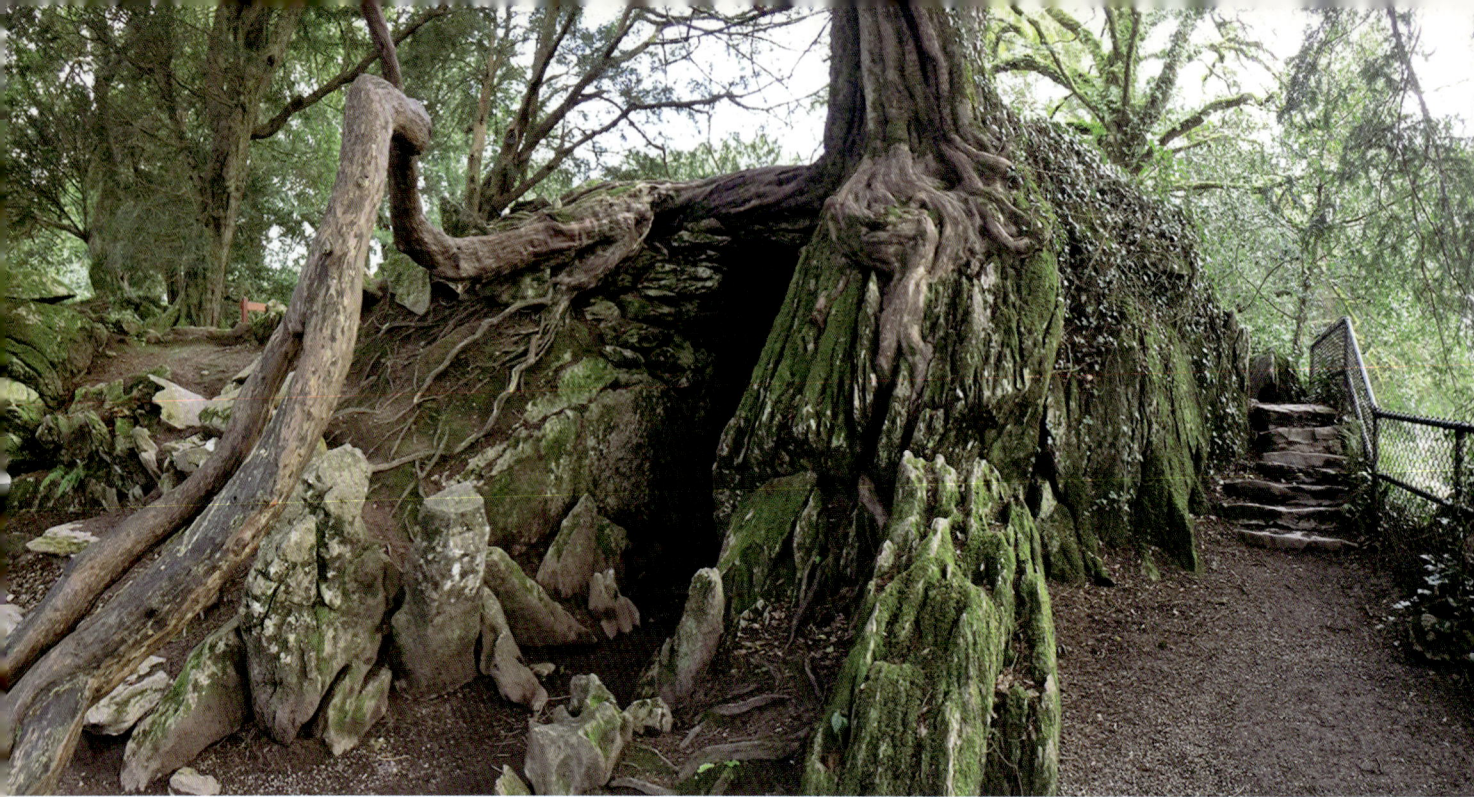

THE ROCK CLOSE

Perhaps the most extraordinary part of the garden is its oldest, the Rock Close, the first stop on the circuit on the eastern side of the Castle.

The Rock Close is a mystical place, said to be the site of an ancient druidic settlement. Shaded by a leafy canopy of ancient yew trees, this part of the garden has a feeling of magic. Most of the curious rocks stand today as they have stood for over 2,000 years, though some arrangements were created by the Jefferyes family in the 1750s as a fitting response to the natural features of the area and to the gaunt old Castle itself.

In this mysterious and hidden landscape are a druidic sacrificial altar, a hermit's cell, a witch's kitchen and other features beneath ancient yew trees, with roots clinging to the bare rock like the veins on a witch's arm. It is said that the yew over the Witch's Kitchen is more than 1,000 years old.

Go all the way into the Witch's Kitchen and see her hearth and chimney. Imagine you have caught a glimpse of the hermit said to have been employed by the Jefferyes family to give their guests the shivers. The vast Dolmen (an ancient burial place marked by one great stone, supported by two others) is thought to be prehistoric.

Then there are the stones of the witch's staircase which will grant your wish IF you perform the necessary ritual CORRECTLY! Beware of the witch's stone. Witches, as we have seen, have mysterious powers. And finally you are advised not to approach the druid's altar when dusk falls....

ABOVE Ancient yew over the entrance to the Witch's Kitchen

OPPOSITE, CLOCKWISE FROM TOP LEFT
The Witch's Kitchen; the magic Witch's Stone; the Dolmen; the Wishing Steps

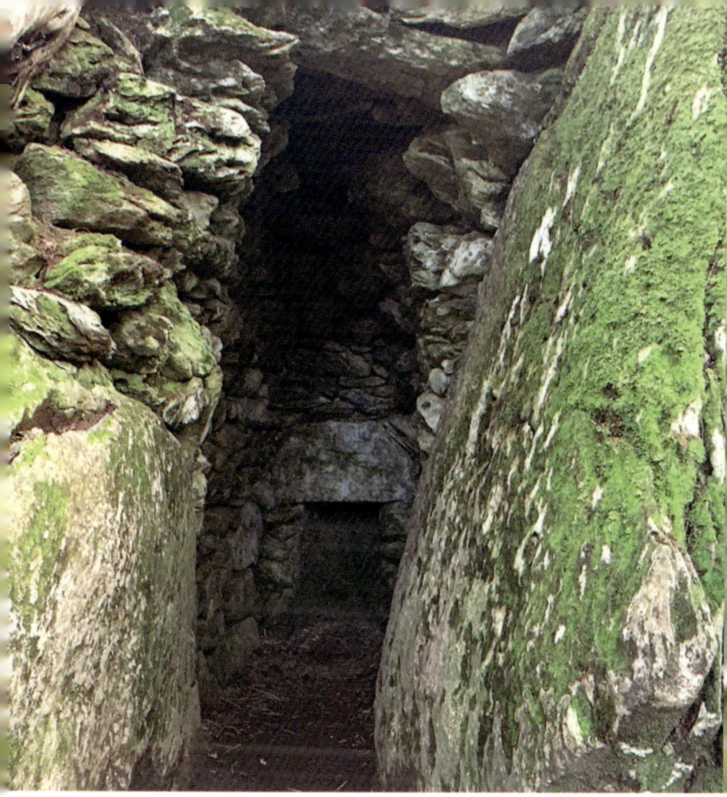

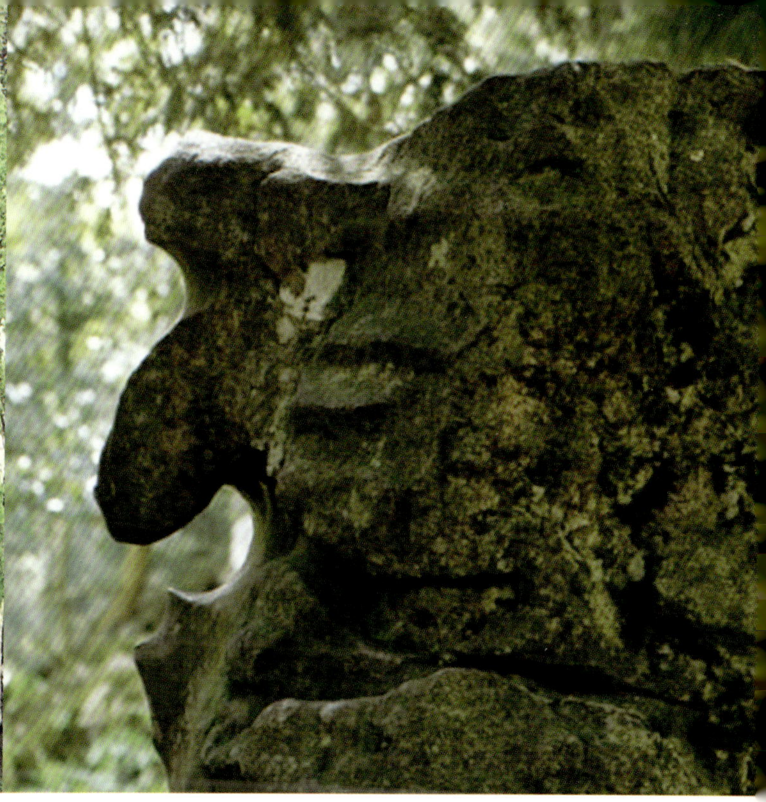

'*It is indeed a fairy scene, and I know of no place where I could sooner imagine these little elves holding their moon-light revelry.*'

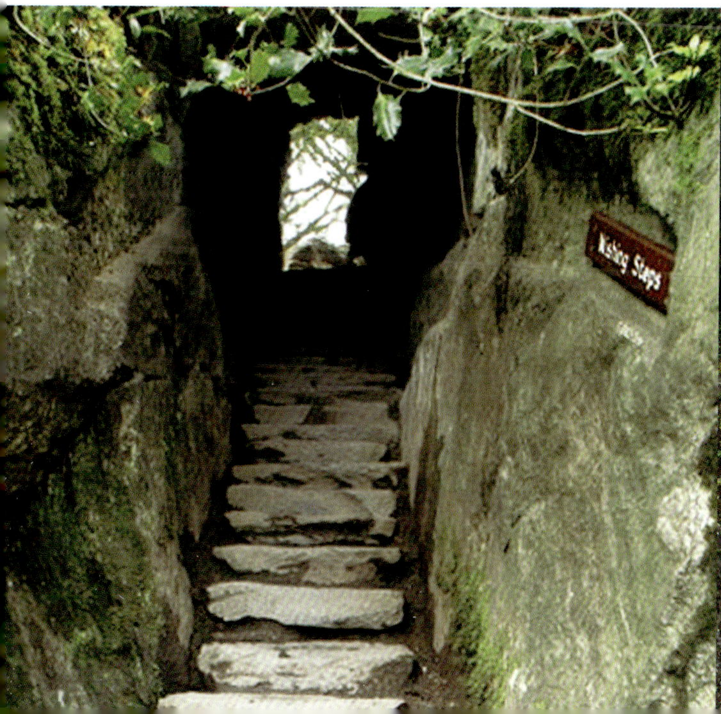

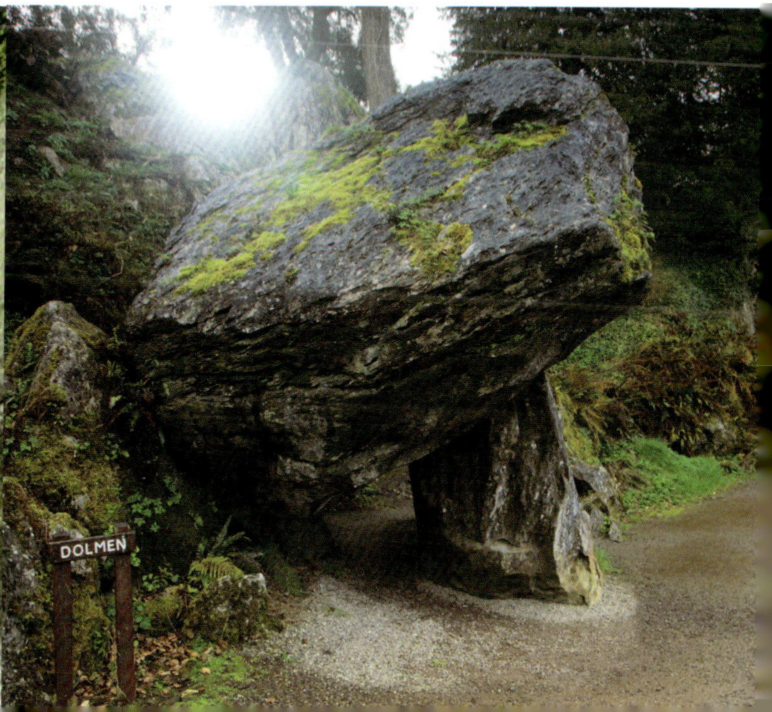

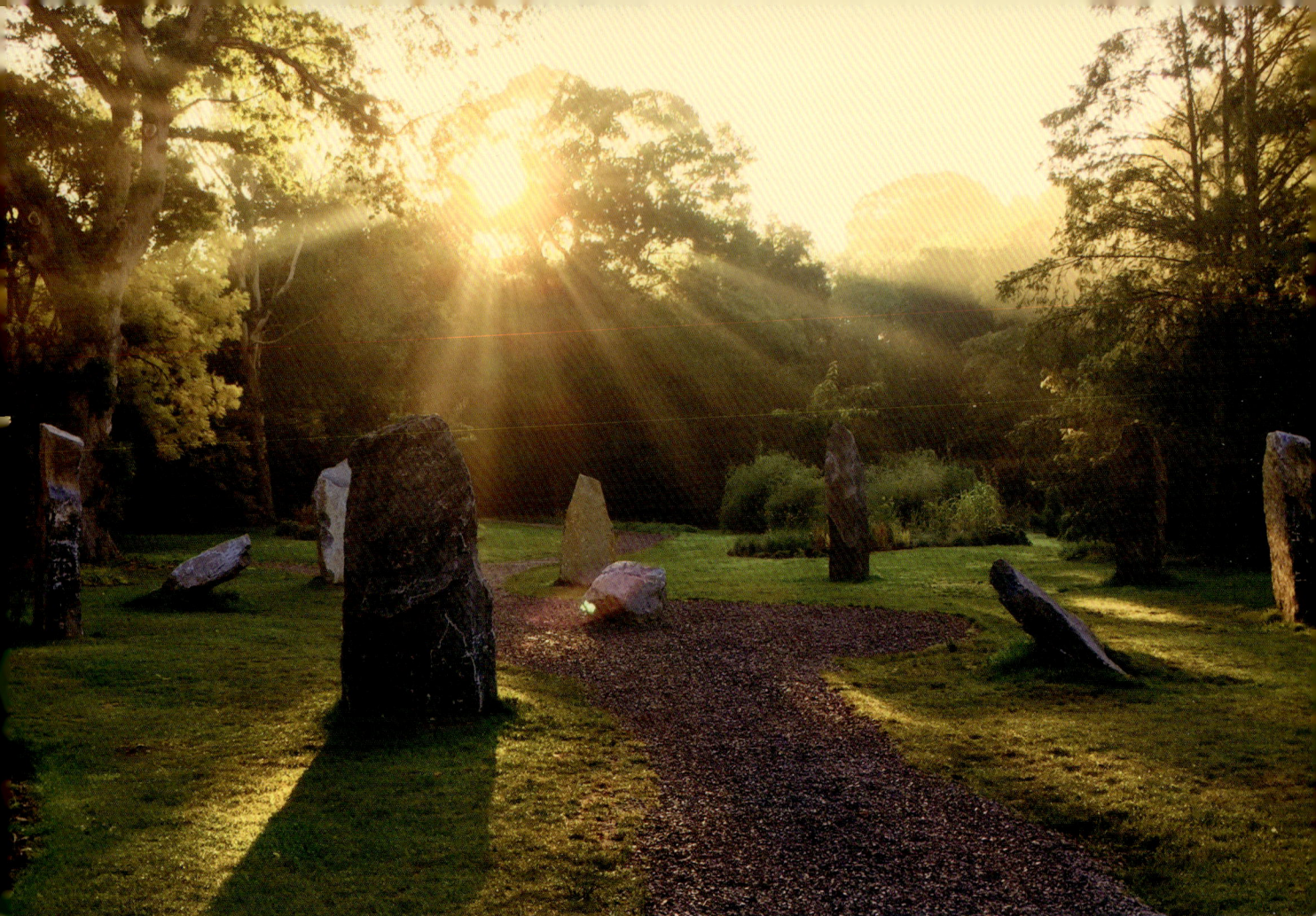

The Seven Sisters

The Blarney Stone is not the only stone with legends attached to it. Just north-east of the Castle can be found a circle of nine standing stones, two of which have fallen. It is said that in medieval times a chieftain who had two fine young sons and seven daughters took his sons on their first battle against a troublesome neighbour who was constantly raiding his cattle. The chieftain was victorious in the battle but at great cost: both his sons were killed. Returning to his castle with his troops and the bodies of his sons, he stopped at this familiar spot and to mark the death of his sons the grieving chieftain ordered his men to knock over two of the stones.

INSTALLATIONS IN THE GARDENS

The beautiful surroundings of the Blarney estate offer a rich variety of settings for art and sculpture. A permanent sculpture collection, including work by some of Ireland's best artists, is joined every summer by a temporary exhibition of work from all across the country. The sculpture trail and art installations draw visitors to every corner of the garden, to discover surprises in many different settings.

OPPOSITE, CLOCKWISE FROM TOP LEFT

Michelle Maher *Synergy*; Pieter Koning, *Prehistoric Bird*; Cork Textiles, Willow Tunnel yarn installation

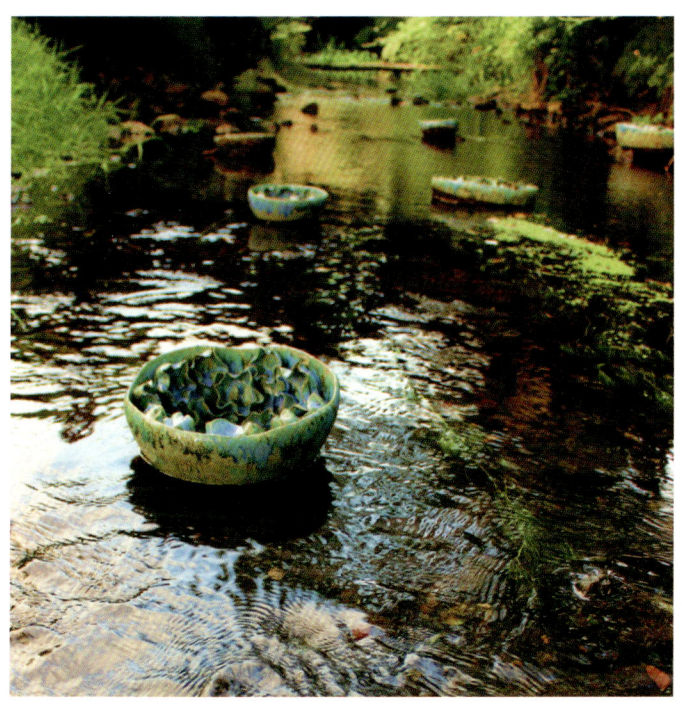
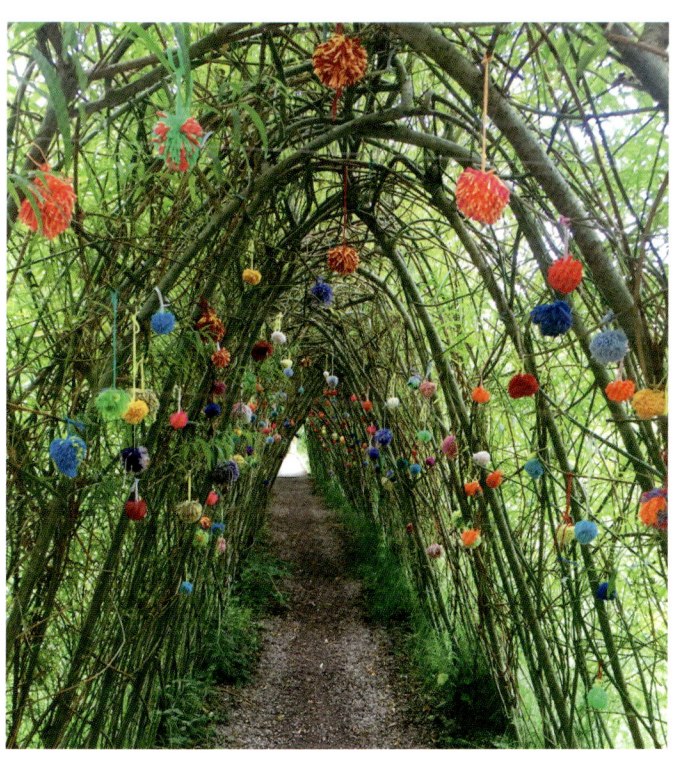

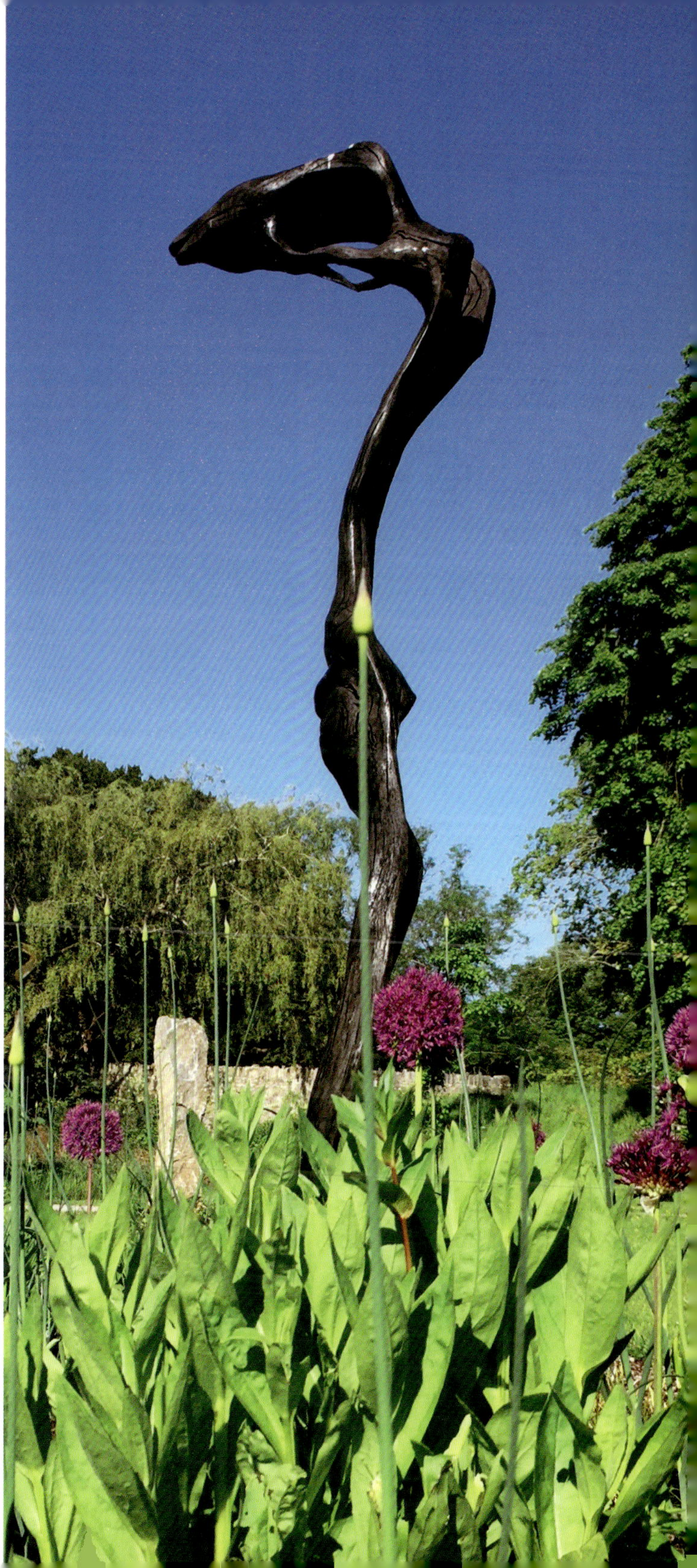

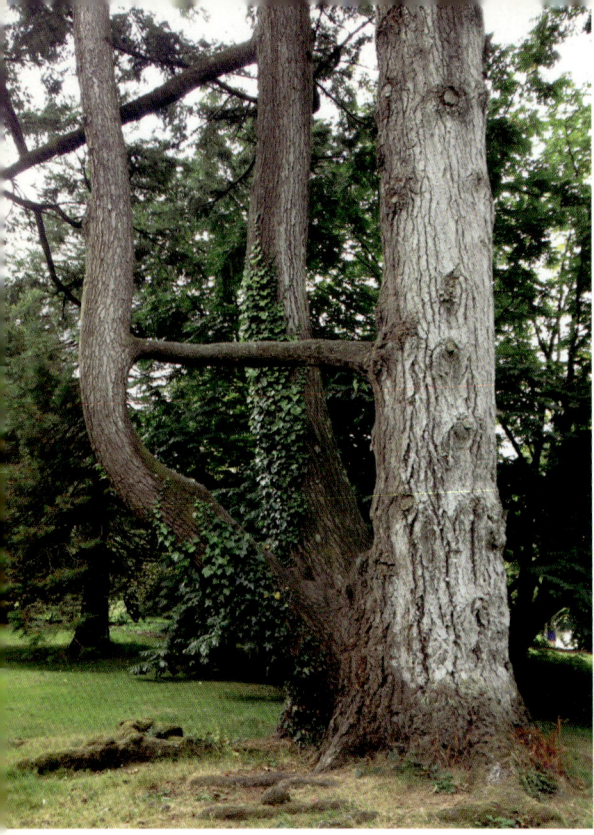

GREAT TREES

The gardens at Blarney Castle contain an exceptional collection of specimen trees, some the largest of their kind in Ireland. Many of the rare trees, such as the foxglove tree (*Paulownia tomentosa*) and the tree of heaven (*Ailanthus altissima*) were planted in the 1970s and 1980s, but many of the limes, cedars and chestnuts are much older – some of them hundreds of years old. The evergreen oaks (*Quercus ilex*) overhanging the Fairy Glade and the Druids' Altar and Stone Circle, are almost 300 years old, and the yews in the Rock Close are even older. Our most photographed tree is the gigantic Western red cedar (*Thuja plicata*), planted in the 1900s, with branches bigger than many full-sized trees, while the Monterey pine (*Pinus radiata*) may be the tallest in Ireland.

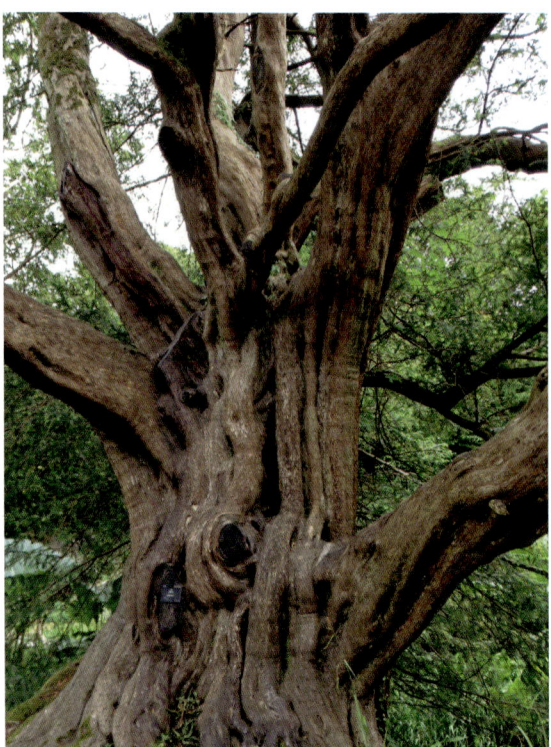

ABOVE LEFT Douglas fir, *Pseudotsuga menziesii* with a natural graft resembling an Irish harp

BELOW LEFT The Elephant Tree, Western red cedar, *Thuja plicata*

LEFT Yew, *Taxus baccata*, said to be over 1,000 years old

OPPOSITE Ancient beech, *Fagus sylivatica*

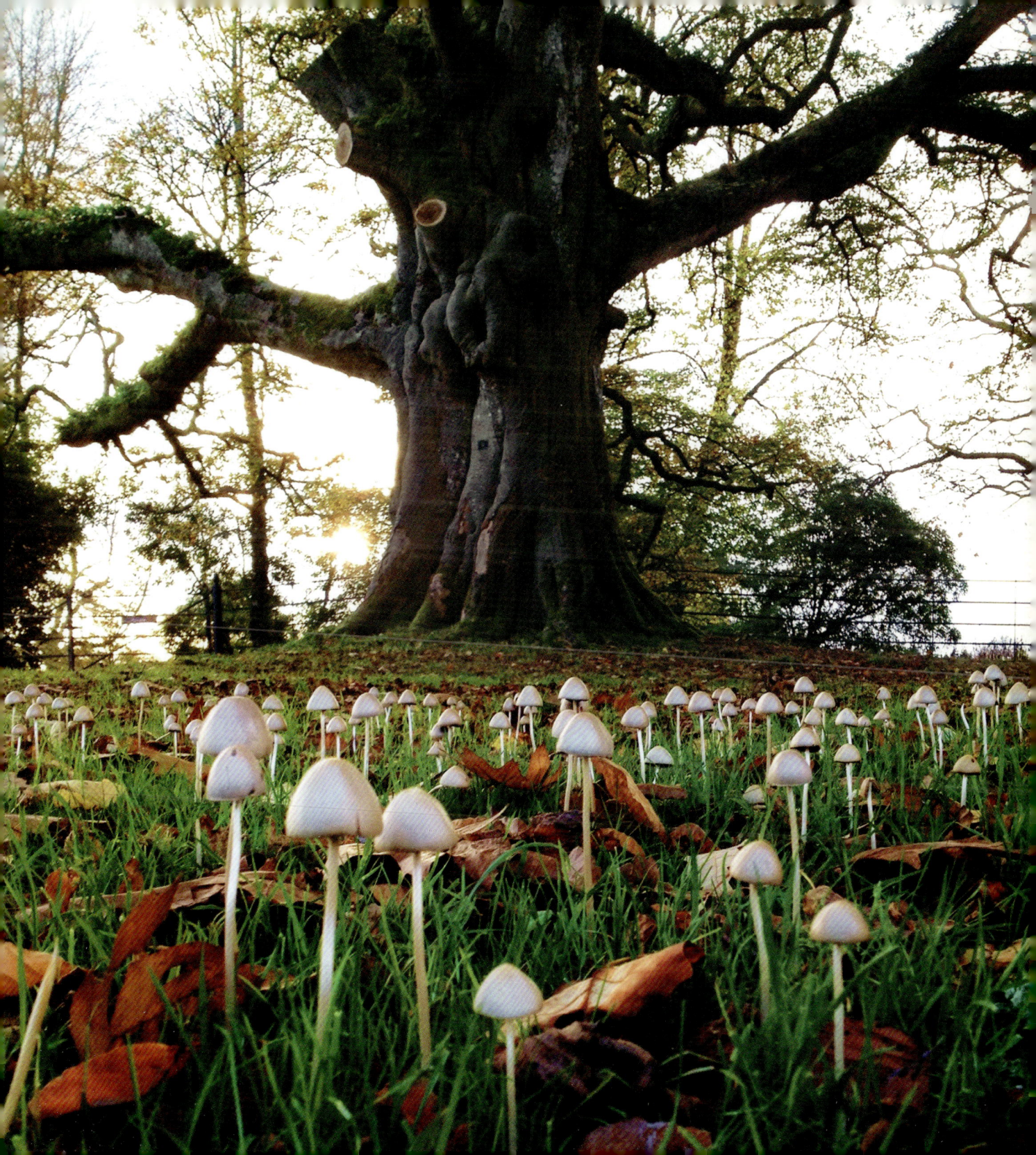

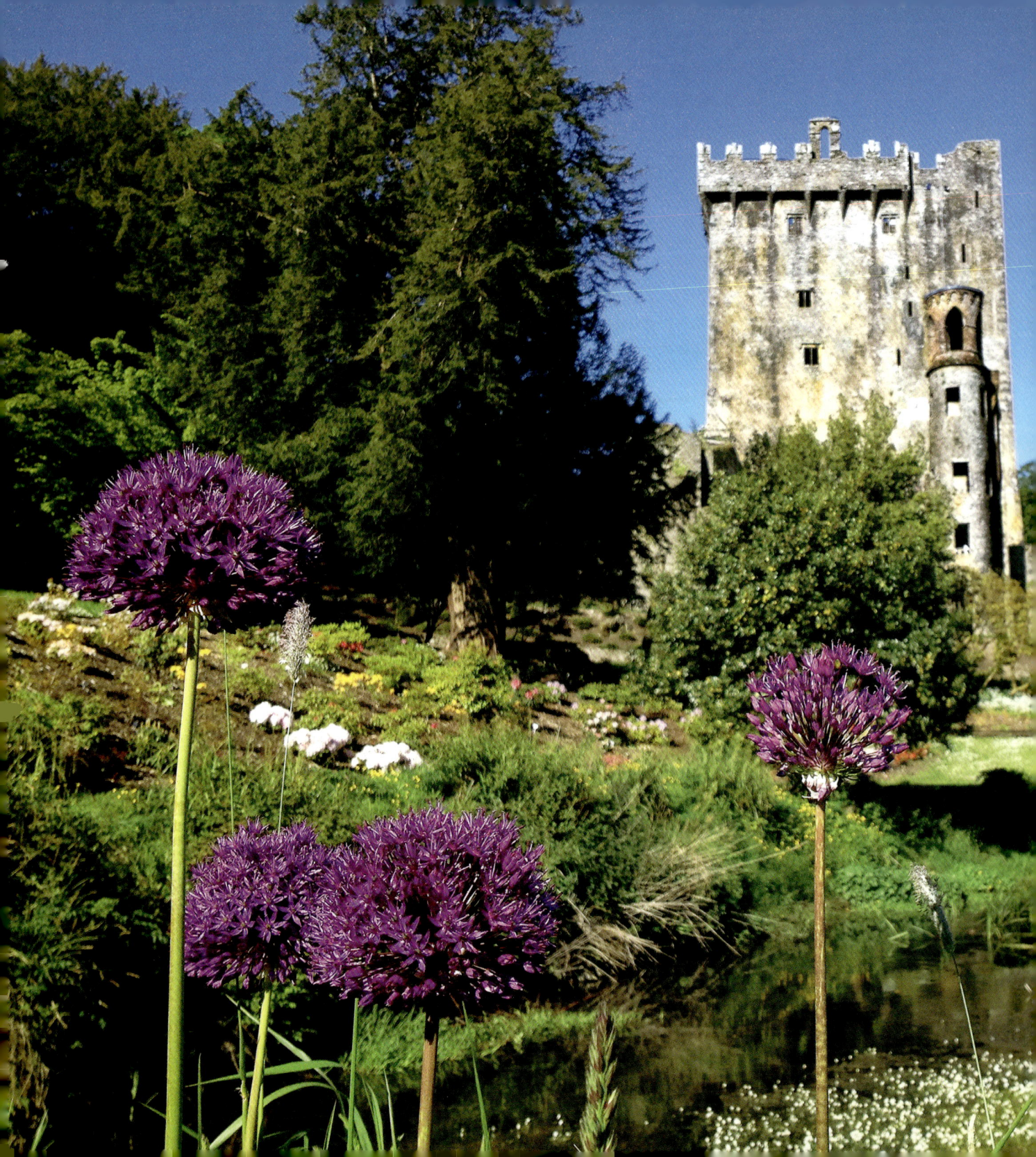

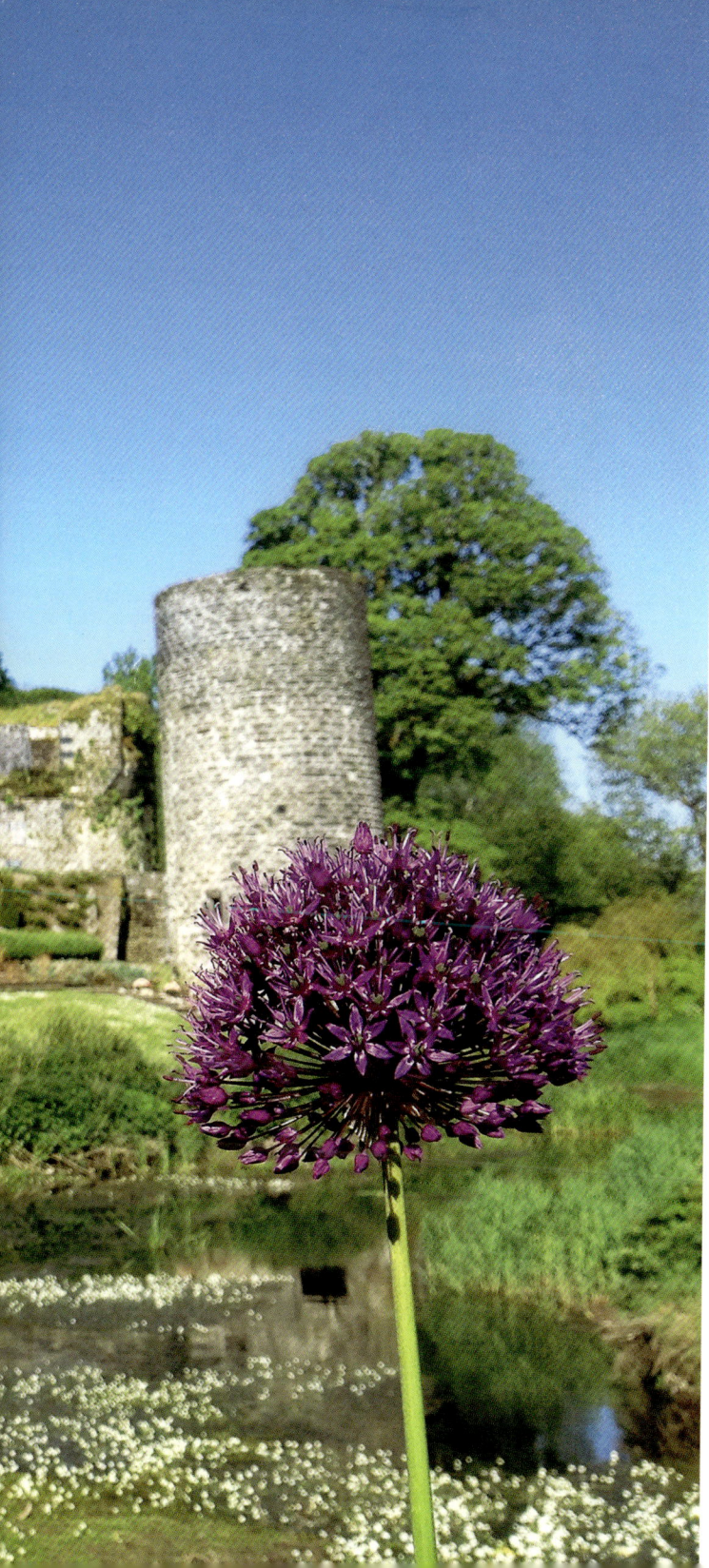

Alliums in bloom on the east side of the Castle

CONSERVATION AT BLARNEY

Blarney Gardens has built an international reputation in the horticultural world as a progressive and professional organisation, and has recently been accepted as a member of Botanic Gardens Conservation International. Blarney Castle & Gardens takes conservation very seriously and has established collections of rare and endangered native plants, working in conjunction with the National Botanic Gardens as well as with other overseas organisations to create ex-situ collections of particularly endangered plant species from countries such as Vietnam.

The estate also boasts an impressive range of native wildlife. Blarney Castle & Gardens is the first estate in Ireland to be awarded the prestigious title of 'Wildlife Estate' by the European Landowners' Organisation. The native woodlands, meadows, rivers and lake within the inner estate, and also in the separate pockets of ground around the village area, provide support for many increasingly rare species, including otters, red squirrels, badgers, barn owls, buzzards, kingfishers, river lampreys, trout and salmon. The whole estate is managed with the aim of creating and improving habitats in favour of biodiversity, as well as restoring natural conditions where species can thrive.

Blarney Castle & Gardens is a unique estate and an extremely valuable asset to both Blarney and County Cork.

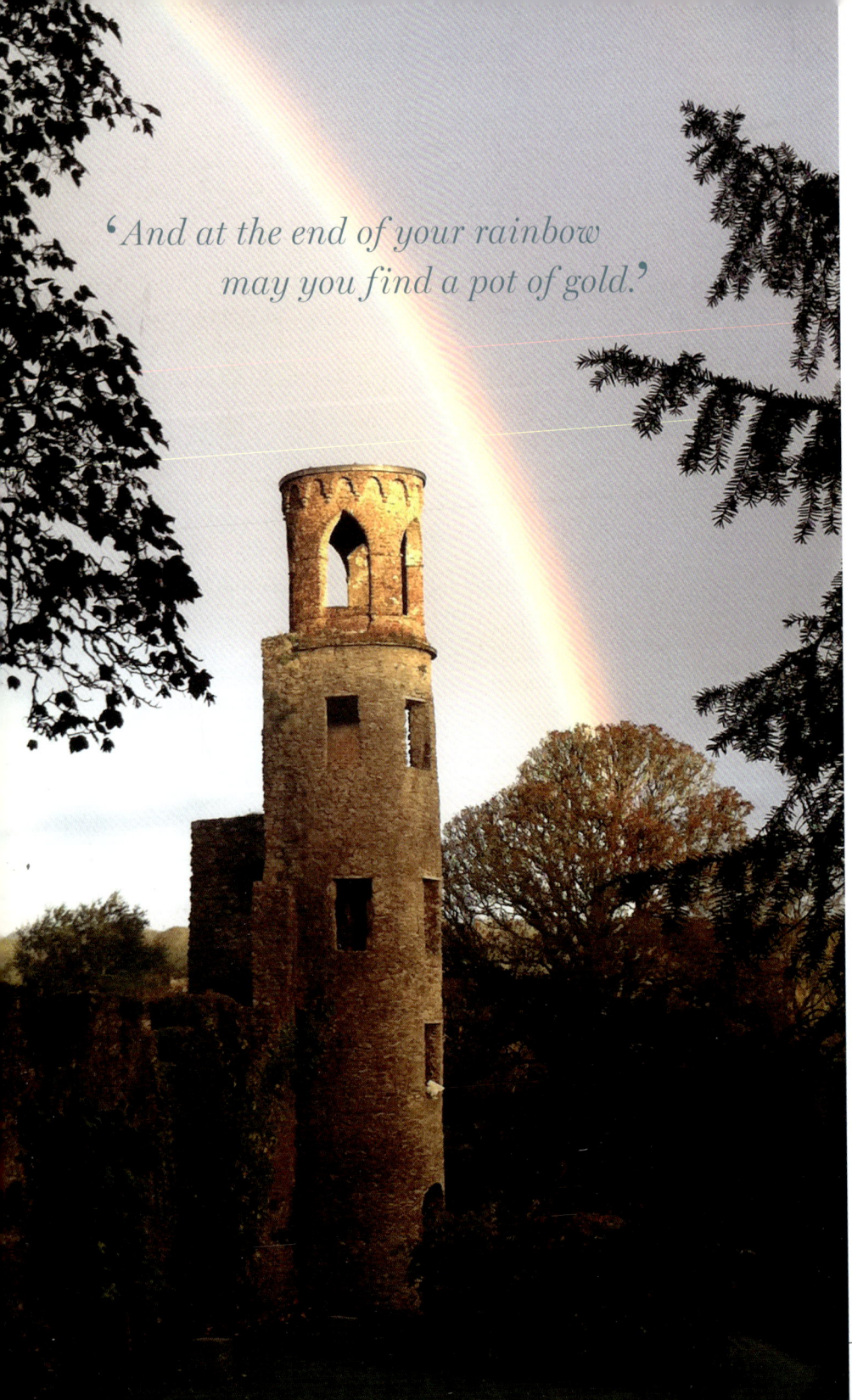

'And at the end of your rainbow may you find a pot of gold.'

This edition © Scala Arts & Heritage Publishers Ltd, 2017
Text and illustrations © Blarney Castle & Gardens, 2017

First published in 2017 by
Scala Arts & Heritage Publishers Ltd
10 Lion Yard, Tremadoc Road
London SW4 7NQ, UK
www.scalapublishers.com

In association with
Blarney Castle & Gardens
Blarney, County Cork
Ireland
www.blarneycastle.ie

ISBN 978-1-78551-082-3

We are grateful to Richard Wood for his contribution to the text.

Edited by Johanna Stephenson
Designed by Ray Watkins
Printed in China

10 9 8 7 6 5 4 3 2 1

All rights reserved. No part of this book may be reproduced, stored in a retrieval system or transmitted in any form or by any means electronic, mechanical, photocopying, recording or otherwise, without the written permission of Blarney Castle & Gardens and Scala Arts & Heritage Publishers Ltd.

Every effort has been made to acknowledge correct copyright of images where applicable. Any errors or omissions are unintentional and should be notified to the Publisher, who will arrange for corrections to appear in any reprints.

PICTURE CREDITS

Page 6: photo David Whooley, 2015 / CC-BY-SA-4.0; page 7, top: W.F. Wakeman, *Wakeman's handbook of Irish antiquities*, Dublin 1903; page 7, bottom: J. Mitchel, *The life and times of Aodh O'Neill, Prince of Ulster*, New York 1868; page 8, left: © National Library of Ireland; page 9, right: © The Hunt Museum, Limerick; page 10, left: by permission of the Royal Irish Academy © RIA; pages 10–11: courtesy of Irish Heritage Trust; page 11, top: © Irish Architectural Archive; pages 11; bottom, 12, 15 bottom: photographs by Margaret Lantry, courtesy of the Blarney Castle Estate; page 19, Pop duo Jedward by Robyn Gallagher / CC BY-SA 3.0; Tara Reid in 2007 by Robin Wong / CC BY 2.5; Laurel and Hardy, *The Flying Deuces* (1939) by RKO / Wikimedia Commons; Alicia Markova Collection, Howard Gotlieb Archival Research Center at Boston University; Ronald Wilson Reagan / Wikimedia Commons; *Sir Walter Scott*, portrait by Sir Henry Raeburn / Wikimedia Commons; Mick Jagger by Georges Biard / CC BY-SA 3.0; Katherine Jenkins by David Skinner / CC BY 2.0; p. 22, *Spring*, 1565 by Pieter Breugel the Elder / Wikimedia Commons.